THE LANGUAGE OF FLOWERS 1550-1680

THE LANGUAGE OF FLOWERS 1550-1680

*Four floral dictionaries
translated from the French,
with an introduction and notes*

RACHEL HENRY

Sphinx House

ALSO BY RACHEL HENRY:

The Language of Flowers and the Victorian Garden

Published by Sphinx House Publishing, Norfolk

Contents

1

INTRODUCTION

HOW IT STARTED

In 2014, while on holiday in Cornwall, we stopped to have lunch in a small market town. As we walked back to the car, we passed an antique shop and went in to browse. Lying on one of the shelves, between some brass candlesticks and a small pottery bowl, was a little book. Measuring just 3½ by 4 inches, and bound in brown mottled boards with a simple brown morocco spine, it clearly had some age to it. Its title page proclaimed it to be *The Floral Dictionary or Language of Flowers* by Anna Maria Campbell. As a lover of old books, I couldn't resist it. I had no idea of the journey it would take me on!

At the time, I knew almost nothing about the language of flowers and, reading through the book, I was fascinated to see quite a number of flowers that I'd never heard of. Were these, I wondered, plants that had gone out of fashion since Victorian times? Had they been a common sight in Victorian gardens? It was that thought – and the research following on from it – that led me to write *The Language of Flowers and the Victorian Garden.*

MORE QUESTIONS THAN ANSWERS

Another thing that interested me was that Anna Maria Campbell specified the colour of each flower that she listed. Was this, I wondered, something that all floral dictionaries did? I investigated some other versions of the language of flowers – and was astonished. Because not only did other lists show some plants that weren't on Anna Maria's (and omit others that were) – but quite a few of the meanings given were different. For example, Anna Maria gives rose campion the meaning of 'polite, graceful' whereas other books say it represents 'love's messengers', 'only deserve my love', 'gentility' or 'you are without pretension'.

How then, I wondered, could this language have been used? An accurate reading of a message would necessitate both sender and recipient having the same book. So did the suitor send a copy of the book along with the bouquet? And how could he be certain that his beloved would identify the flowers correctly? Could she, for example, distinguish between an ivy geranium ('bridal favour'), an oak geranium ('true friendship') and a nutmeg geranium ('an expected meeting')? Maybe she would think she was receiving an offer of marriage when, in fact, the message was 'you're a good friend' or even 'I'll see you on Tuesday as arranged'.

So it seemed to me that the idea of 'bouquets with meanings' was just not feasible. And, as I started to investigate, I found that others had come to this conclusion before me. In *The Language of Flowers: A History* by Beverly Seaton (University of Virginia Press, 2012), the author writes *"There is almost no evidence that people actually used these symbolic lists to communicate, even if the parties agreed upon what book to use for their meanings".*

Beverly Seaton was not the first person to express such thoughts. In an issue of *The Spectator* published on February 3rd 1866, an anonymous reviewer of the recently published *Language and Sentiment of Flowers. Compiled and edited by 'L.V.'* wrote:

In the first place there is no "language of flowers". To justify such a phrase, there ought to be in all countries a well understood relation between certain visible qualities in the flower and human sentiment, which relation should not vary except with a change in the nature of the flower itself. Of course no such cipher exists, for the signs upon which it is to be based are not universally, or indeed very widely, distributed ... Moreover, much of the "language" is based not upon qualities in the flower, but on its name, and there is for a very natural reason no division of human speech so infinitely various as the names of flowers. They have been named almost universally by the people, whose idea of a new word is always something descriptive, as maidenhair, pheasant's eye, or sunflower ... The aspen signifies fear everywhere, because everywhere it shakes, but the "shepherd's purse" can be and is the symbol of wealth only in Great Britain.

The reviewer also questions the reason why anyone should use such a 'cipher' rather than plain words, either written or spoken:

It has never been put to serious use, and indeed never can be,
for it lacks the two first elements of a good cipher, secrecy and
the capacity of conveying either address or signature.

And he (I suspect it was written by a man) also wonders why certain phrases would ever need to be delivered in a secretive way:

"Cheerfulness in old age" - American starwort - is not
a sentiment it is useful to convey in cipher, and if one
is talking one may as well say, "The variety of your
conversation delights me," as present a clarkia . . . Most
people, too, would be slow to present a grammanthus
chloraflora if it really means "Your temper is too hasty".

The point about the language of flowers being a cipher which lacks secrecy is an important one, and one that had, several decades earlier, been expressed in an article by the Austrian orientalist and historian Joseph von Hammer-Purgstall (1774-1856). Translated into English, the article was published in various journals including *The Classical Journal* in 1814 and *The Monthly Messenger* in 1840. By the time of the latter printing, the language of flowers had become very popular in both England and France and, in England in particular, it was believed by many to have developed from a version used in Turkish harems.

The origin of this belief arose from a letter sent in 1716 by Lady Mary Wortley Montagu who, between 1716 and 1718, accompanied her diplomat husband in his travels through the Ottoman Empire. Her letters were published in book form and, such was the interest in them, that they have remained in print to the present day.

"I have got for you," writes Lady Mary to her friend, *"a Turkish love-letter, which I have put into a little box."* The 'letter' consists of eighteen items – not all flowers or plants but including things such as paper, soap, coal and gold thread. Indeed, Lady Mary goes on to say:

There is no colour, no flower, no weed, no fruit, herb, pebble, or feather, that has not a verse belonging to it; and you may quarrel, reproach, or send letters of passion, friendship, or civility, or even of news, without ever inking your fingers.

The examples she gives are:

Ingi *Pearl*
Sensin Guzelerin gingi
Fairest of the young.

Caremfil *Clove*
Caremfilsen cararen yok
You are as slender as the clove!

Pul *Jonquil*
Derdime derman bul
Have pity on my passion!

Kihat *Paper*
Birlerum sahat sahat
I faint every hour!

Ermus   *Pear*

Ver bize bir umut

Give me some hope.

Jabun   *Soap*

Derdinden oldum zabun

I am sick with love.

Chemur   *Coal*

Ben oliyim size umur

May I die, and all my years be yours!

Gul   *A rose*

Ben aglarum sen gul

May you be pleased, and your sorrows mine!

Hasir   *A straw*

Oliim sana yazir

Suffer me to be your slave.

Jo ha   *Cloth*

Ustune bulunmaz pahu

Your price is not to be found.

Tartsin   *Cinnamon*

Sen ghel ben chekeim senin hargin

But my fortune is yours.

Gira *A match*
Esking-ilen oldum ghira
I burn, I burn! my flame consumes me!

Sirma *Gold thread*
Uzunu benden a yirma
Don't turn away your face.

Satch *Hair*
Bazmazum tatch
Crown of my head!

Uzum *Grape*
Benim iki Guzum
My eyes!

Tel *Gold wire*
Ulugorum tez ghel
I die — come quickly.

And, by way of postscript:

Biber *Pepper*
Bize bir dogm haber
Send me an answer.

It will be immediately obvious that, unlike the meanings given to many flowers in traditional Western floral dictionaries, most of these Turkish meanings seem to have no association with the form of the object or flower itself or with its mythology. Rather, it is all to do with rhyme. The last word of the meaning either rhymes or assonates with the object - ingi and gingi, pul and bul, kihat and sahat, jabun and zabun, jo ha and pahu, and so on.

Joseph von Hammer-Purgstall, writing nearly a hundred years after Lady Mary Wortley Montagu, begins his article by commenting that few of his readers can be unaware that *"there exists a certain mysterious language of love and gallantry, which expresses by means of flowers the most delicate and tender sentiments."* But:

> *All the information which we have hitherto acquired on this subject, chiefly derived from romances, or books of travels much resembling romances, seemed so vague and imperfect, that we resolved to rectify it by examining its very source.*

He acknowledges that *"the sixteen phrases, which compose the amorous epistle* [sent by Lady Mary Wortley Montagu], *are translated with sufficient accuracy"* but goes on to say:

> *We know nothing that resembles it among the other Oriental nations, from Persia to China, or from Tartary to India . . . It is then in Turkey alone, and even there only in the harems, that we find this mysterious language.*

And it is here that he parts company with those who believed that this 'language' was used to pass messages between the women of the harem and their lovers outside their confining walls:

*It can never be a sure medium of correspondence between
the harems and those without their precincts. A language
understood by all the world could not, by any means, answer
the purposes of two lovers, whose lives would be forfeited on
the slightest discovery of a mutual understanding.*

The difficulty faced by *"common mortals"* wishing to communicate in
any way with those enclosed in harems and guarded by eunuchs cannot
be underestimated, says Hammer-Purgstall. And this is not the only
problem. Even supposing that:

> *by an extraordinary combination of good fortune and
> discretion, a lover should find means of corresponding, in
> spite of walls and eunuchs, with the lady of his affections,
> would he employ a visible language, the secret of which is not
> only in the porter's hands, but known to all the eunuchs, and
> all the fair rivals who might see the nosegay? – or, if this
> language was not generally understood, how could the lover
> imagine that his mistress, lately arrived perhaps from the
> frontier of Circassia, or of Abyssinia, should comprehend
> his meaning?*

The 'language of flowers' he concludes, cannot be *"a love-cypher
for billet-doux between men and women who wish to carry on a secret
correspondence"*. However, he goes on to assure his readers that this
doesn't mean that such a language doesn't exist. On the contrary, it does
exist but its use and its vocabulary are much more limited than popular
legend would suggest:

It has been invented by [the harem women] in the leisure
hours of their solitary life, and they use it either as a mere
amusement, or as a cypher to express the violent affections
which they frequently entertain for one another . . . The
dictionary of it cannot be voluminous : in fact we do not
know that any exists, although, during a residence of several
years at Constantinople, we made every necessary inquiry.
The whole treasury of this language does not much exceed
a hundred signs and received phrases . . . as we learned . .
. from the Greek and Armenian women who had frequent
opportunities of visiting the interior of the harems.

Quite clearly the Victorian language of flowers bore little relationship
to Lady Mary Wortley Montagu's 'cipher'. But where did it come from?
Was it invented by an individual, inspired by the legend of this cipher?
Or was it an ancient oral tradition that found its way into print during
the Victorian era? My curiosity was piqued!

I START TO FIND SOME ANSWERS

My questions were partly answered when I discovered *Abécédaire de*
Flore ou Langage des Fleurs by B. Delachenaye, published in Paris in
1811. In the introduction, the author comments that *"Before letters were*
invented, men transmitted their thoughts through images". He then goes
on to mention an event in 1729, when *"according to Father Menestrier*
. . . a carousel was made at the court of Savoy, where the flowers competed
for the honour of crowning the Princess of Piedmont on her feast day. Each
knight took the name of a flower, and a similar motto".

Delachenaye was writing around the same time as Joseph von Hammer-Purgstall but it is unlikely that he had read the essay which I quoted above because he goes on to express his belief in the existence of the 'selam', *"a small bundle of flowers, fruits, wood, and other objects, all of which have an allegorical meaning"* which he says is used *"in Turkey and throughout the Orient".* The examples he produces to back up this belief, however, come only from romantic fiction. But he seems to believe that the authors of these stories had knowledge of a true Oriental cipher and he laments that Bernardin de Saint-Pierre (1737-1814) author of the novel *La Chaumière Indienne* (The Indian Cottage), published in 1790, *"did not undertake to compose a complete method of such a desired language."* But such lists apparently did exist, for he tells us:

> *For some years we have seen catalogues or lists of flowers, accompanied by significations, which offer the most piquant and delicate allusions to the characters of persons and to passions in general.*

These lists, however, differ from one another and this leads Delachenaye to believe that:

> *these productions, without pretension as without authority, do not come from a real source, and there is a great risk of deceiving oneself if one believes that one finds in these lists the true meaning used in Oriental language.*

The lists, he says, *"first written by hand, and rare for this reason, are already propagated by printing"* although his is the earliest book of this period that I have been able to track down, and I suspect that the printed lists to which he refers are just that – lists or pamphlets – rather than books.

So it seemed likely that the compilers of these lists, possibly inspired by stories of the 'selam' decided to create a Western version – which seemed to answer my question about the origins of the language of flowers.

And there it would have remained, but for the fact that I was still researching individual floral dictionaries. When I wrote *The Language of Flowers and the Victorian Garden* I referred to 14 of these. Were there more, I wondered? By the time I sat down to write the series of which the present volume will be the first, I had discovered about 150, some of them – like Anna Maria Campbell's which had started my quest – quite rare. And it was towards the end of this period of research that – to my astonishment and delight – I discovered a French floral dictionary from the 17th century and then, researching that, another from the 16th century.

There, however, it stops. The first of these books, dating to 1558, was published scarcely 100 years after the introduction of moveable type into Europe. Although I attempted to trace something earlier, I was unsuccessful. There may have been handwritten versions but, if so, these have not survived. None of these early books gives any indication of where the lists have come from but, as you will see in the main part of this book, they are included in volumes concerned with heraldry (and thus emblems) and with games and fortune telling. I have been unable to discover any particular use of flowers in heraldry at this time (other than the ones that are well known, such as the fleur de lys and the rose) so it is unlikely that the meanings were derived from anything heraldic, although it is possible that the idea of using flowers as emblems or symbols may have been inspired by heraldry.

As to fortune telling, this has been popular since ancient times, and it may well be that the use of flowers for divination gradually evolved into a 'language'.

Unfortunately, there seems to be no connection between the 16th and 17th century dictionaries and those of the 19th century. As far as I have been able to ascertain none of the later listings bears any resemblance to the earlier ones. Whether any floral dictionaries were published in the intervening years, or whether the idea lost popularity for 100 years or so, I have been unable to discover.

AN INTERESTING REVELATION

However, one of my beliefs that I mentioned at the start of this Introduction – that it seemed impossible for the listings ever to have been used as a real language of flowers, with bouquets conveying hidden meanings – has been thrown into doubt by the earliest of these books, *La Recreation et Devis d'Amours*, published in 1558. It contains, at the start of the book, 18 questions and answers about love and romance and, among these, we find:

> *Why do lovers often adorn their beloved's door with beautiful twigs, mays and hats of flowers?*

(Father François Pomey's *Le Dictionaire Royal*, published in 1680, defines 'may' as 'a tree that is planted at the doors of the houses'.)

The answer to this question tells us that:

> *those who want to honour something sacred or some divine temple, often plant many beautiful branches in front of these places . . . Thus a lover, loving above all things the*

beauty of his lady, often in front of her door honours her in
this way, to demonstrate his feelings towards her.

This answers another point which has been raised against the language of flowers, as it stands, being used for messages – the appearance of fruit and vegetables in the listings. After all, who has ever included a potato or a turnip or even an apple in a bouquet. But if there was a tradition of leaving 'offerings' outside the loved one's door, this becomes more credible.

The second earliest volume I found (published in 1579) also provides a list of different ways to tie a bouquet – the different coloured threads or ribbons having different meanings – and this, too, suggests that, at least in the 16th century, these meanings were understood and used to send messages.

As far as meanings are concerned, those of the four floral dictionaries that I have reproduced in this book are much the same as each other, so there is likely to have been much less confusion as to the message being sent than there would have been if one had tried to use one of the numerous versions of the 19th century.

2

THE BOOKS

Although the books on which this volume is based have very similar floral dictionaries, they do differ in several other respects so I will treat them (plus one other) individually in this section in order to put the dictionary into context.

I am not an expert in mediaeval French so it's possible that I may have missed the odd nuance when translating. However, wherever possible, I have checked the meaning of unfamiliar words and phrases in dictionaries published in the same period or slightly later.

LA RECREATION ET DEVIS D'AMOURS 1558

This is the earliest of the books. Its full title is: *La Recreation et Devis d'Amours, avec les demandes amoureuses. Le tout composé au contentement & plaisir de tous vrays amans.* It was published in Lyon by Benoit Rigaud and Jean Saugrain in 1558.

Roughly, the title translates as: *The recreation [or games] and speech of love, with amorous requests. The whole composed for the contentment & pleasure of all true lovers.*

It seems that there was an earlier edition (published in 1556) but, as I have not seen it, I cannot say whether the 1558 version is a reprint or a new edition. No author is identified.

The book begins with a short verse:
He who wants to play in love
To use the right words to laugh
And to satisfy the ladies
He needs to read this delightful discourse.

After this, there's a list of 18 questions and answers on the subject of love. These include:

What is the cause of lovers not being able to sleep at night?
Why can't sleeping lovers always dream of their loved ones?
Why do lovers happily carry bouquets, golden apples and other beautiful fruits?
And the question already mentioned in the Introduction, above:
Why do lovers often adorn their beloved's door with beautiful twigs, trees and hats of flowers?

The next section consists of an eight-line verse and then two longer poems. The first of these is entitled *L'auteur aux dames* [The author to the ladies] and the second is *Les devis amoureux* [Amorous speech] which takes the form of a dialogue between a lover and his beloved.

After this comes *Le blason des herbes, arbres et fleurs* – the floral dictionary.

A four line verse following the floral dictionary addresses the readers:
Ladies, take great heed
Of these emblems with satisfaction
Which are according your bidding,
[And which] you send in place of writing.

After which comes a series of questions and responses including:
Q. I ask you, if love had lost its name, what would you call it?
A. Pleasant wisdom
Q. How do lovers hear what they long for?
A. Humbly request and pray
Q. In which month are lovers sickest?
A. In the month of May
Q. What often makes love last?
A. Courtesy

A second series of questions and responses is entitled: *Other love requests, which knights-at-arms and other people of honour may request from each other, and the responses made to each request, and all are proved by reasons. And first the knight asks the lady and she answers him point by point in the following manner.*

The way in which this is expressed suggests that the author may be thinking in terms of courtly love, a mediaeval concept which the British Library website describes as being *"characterised by a series of stylised rituals between a knight and a married lady of high rank . . . based on the traditional codes of conduct associated with knighthood, such as duty, honour, courtesy and bravery"*.

Further insight into the social mores of the time is offered by some of the answers to the questions. The knight asks the lady whether a woman is as jealous as a man. She replies that a woman is more jealous because men are free to travel and to meet (and perhaps woo) many women. He then asks which lasts longer, the jealousy of a man or of a woman. Here again, the answer is that it is that of a woman *"for she does not go to so many places and would not dare to speak of her wishes like a man in case she be dishonoured and despised"*.

The man asks 27 questions of the woman, then she asks eight of him, after which the volume concludes with a series of short poems.

LA RECREATION, DEVIS ET MIGNARDISE AMOUREUSE   1579

The full title of the next book is: *La Recreation, Devis et Mignardise Amoureuse. Contenant plusieurs Blasons, menues pensees, Verger, ventes, & demandes de l'amant à l'amie, & autres propos Amoureux.* It was published in Paris by Nicolas Bonfons in 1579.

This title is harder to translate than the first. 'Mignardise' can be translated as 'delicacy' or 'delicate speech' and 'blasons' (which is a heraldic term meaning 'coats of arms') as 'emblems'. But the literal translation of 'verger, ventes' is 'orchard, sales', which is clearly not correct! However, the *Dictionnaire Historique de l'Ancien Langage François* (published in 1882) offers the colloquialism *'ventes d'amour'* which relates to questions and answers between lovers.

So an approximation, perhaps, is: *The recreation [or games], chit-chat and amorous delicate sayings. Containing several emblems, little thoughts, and questions between the lover and his love, and other amorous remarks.*

The Biblioteque Nationale de France identifies the author as Guillaume Des Autels (1529-?1599) and it seems likely that he was also the author of the 1558 book. He was a poet who had studied the humanities and philosophy and, later, law at the University of Valence, although he never practised as a lawyer. He is said to have been a friend of Nostradamus and, while not a major poet, he was influential on the literature of his time. The book begins with *Epistre aux dames* [a letter to the ladies] in which the author introduces his book and this is followed by *La mignardise plaisante d'amour* [Delightful trinkets of love] which is identical to the 18 questions and answers at the start of the 1558 book.

Then come four poems:

Description de la nature d'amour [A description of the nature of love]

Les amoureux devis avec le blason des herbes et fleurs – identical to *Les devis amoureux* in the previous book

Autres ventes plaisantes et recreatives, adjoutees de nouveau [Other delightful and recreational questions, newly added] and

Les menues pensees d'amours [Little thoughts about love]

After this there are two series of questions and answers identical to those in the previous volume. And then we get on to the language of flowers. Now, the only copy I could find of this book contains no floral dictionary. However, I have included the volume here because it contains an essay on *Le blason de la ligature du bouquet* [The meanings of the tying of the bouquet].

Whether the publishers decided to omit the floral dictionary or whether this volume has just lost its final pages in the 450 years since it was printed, I cannot be certain. However, the former seems more likely since, in later editions of the book, the dictionary is specifically mentioned in the title and comes before the essay on tying, not at the end. If the book was, indeed, printed without the floral dictionary this might suggest that, by this time, it was already well known among the sort of people who would have bought this volume and so didn't need to be repeated. Or maybe it was an encouragement for them to buy the earlier book, too. (Marketing is not a modern concept!). Whatever, the case – lost pages or marketing ploy – this volume is of value because of its list of meanings of different bindings:

- *Grass, alone or with thread or silk, indicates that there is no message in the flowers other than the good wishes of the person sending them.*

- *Hair used to tie the bouquet indicates a wish of well-being from the sender, together with his heart, body and soul.*

- *Crude thread straight from the spindle emphasises all the meanings and the sender's expectation of a good or bad response.*

- *White thread, while indicating hope of a good response, doesn't affect the meanings in any way.*

- *Black thread emphasises the positive meanings and asks that anything not fully understood is taken in a positive way; there is an expectation of a good response.*

- *Greenish-blue or blue thread emphasises negative meanings, reduces the value of any positive ones and, needless to say, has no hope of a good response.*

- *Grey thread means the sender has hope of a good response. The meanings are to be read at face value.*

- *Green thread increases the positive meanings, negates any others and hopes for a good response.*

- *Tan thread does not affect the meanings but indicates that the sender has no hope of a good response*

- *Yellow thread emphasises all the meanings.*

- *Violet thread, while not changing the meanings, states that they are true.*

- *Red thread does not affect the meanings but indicates that the sender expects a negative response.*

- *Crimson thread does not affect the meanings and indicates that the sender has no hope of any response whatever.*

- *If the bouquet is tied with silk, rather than linen or other thread, all the meanings implied by the colours are reinforced even more.*

- *Gold and silver thread is to be used only by the nobility, gold when the sender is a man and silver when the sender is a woman. In all cases, the meanings of the flowers are reinforced.*

- *Finally, to indicate that there is no hidden message in the flowers, the sender should tie two knots at each end of the thread.*

LES RECREATIONS, DEVIS ET MIGNARDISES 1625

The full title of this volume is: *Les Recreations, Devis et Mignardises: Demandes & Responces; que les Amoureux font en l'Amour. Avec le*

Blason des herbes & fleurs, pour faire les bouquets. Sonnets, & dizains, fort convenable a ces devis, nouvellement fait au contentement & plaisire de tous vrais Amans. It was published in Lyon by Jean Huguetan in 1625.

Once again, the title of this volume is slightly different from the previous one. It translates roughly as: *The games, chit-chat and delicacies: questions and answers that lovers use in love. With the emblems of plants and flowers, to make bouquets. Sonnets, & verses, very suitable for these conversations, newly made for the satisfaction & pleasure of all true lovers.*

No author is identified for this book but it seems to be based pretty much on the previous two volumes.

The book begins with the same verse that is to be found at the start of the first volume. But there is one difference – in the third line, the word 'contenter' (satisfy) is replaced by 'tourmenter' (tease), so that the poem now reads:

He who wants to play in love
To use the right words to laugh
And to tease the ladies
He needs to read this delightful discourse.

Immediately the book takes on a more light hearted tone! However, much of it remains the same as in previous volumes. It begins with the usual series of questions and answers. Then comes the poem previously called *Les devis amoureux* and now entitled *Les ventes d'amours*. Next, we find *Le blason des herbes, arbres et fleurs* – the floral dictionary – which is followed by *Le blason de la ligature du bouquet* – the meaning in the tying of the bouquet (as in the previous volume). The book concludes with more questions and answers and a poem, all taken from the earlier volumes.

LES ORACLES DIVERTISSANS *with* TRAITÉ CURIEUX ET RECREATIF 1649

The book has now been enlarged and divided into two distinct sections, each with its own title page. The full titles are: *Les Oracles Divertissans, ou l'on Trouve la Decision des Questions les plus curieuses pour se rejouir dans les Compagnies. Avec un traite tres recreatif des Couleurs, aux Armoiries, aux Livrees, & aux Faveurs; & la signification des Plantes, Fleurs, & Fruits.*

and:

Traité Curieux et Recreatif des couleurs & de leurs blazons & symboles mysterieux aux Armoiries, aux Livrees & aux Faveurs; & des devises & signifcations d'amour, d'indifference & de mespris, qui s'expliquent par toute sorte d'Arbres, d'Herbes, & de Fleurs.

The first of these translates as:

Entertaining Oracles where we find answers to the most curious questions to enjoy again in society. With a recreational treatise on Colours, Arms, Liveries, & Favours; & the meaning of Plants, Flowers, & Fruits.

The translation of the second title is:

Curious and Recreational Treatment of colours & their meanings & mysterious symbols in Coats of Arms, Liveries & Favours; & mottoes & meanings of love, indifference & contempt, which are explained by all sorts of Trees, Herbs, & Flowers.

The Biblioteque Nationale de France identifies the author as Marc Vulson de la Colombière (died 1658). He was a member of the Paris parliament and wrote a number of successful books on a variety of subjects including heraldry, symbolism and dreams.

In these two volumes we move much more into the light-hearted world of parlour games and fortune telling and away from the more serious considerations of courtly love.

The first volume begins with a foreword addressed '*aux dames*' [to the ladies] and this is followed by a short preface explaining how to use the fortune-telling question-and-answer game that follows. Despite the foreword being addressed to the ladies, many of the questions seem to be those that a man might ask. However, they are no longer the serious questions posed about the nature of love and lovers that we saw in the previous volumes and are, for the most part, fairly innocuous, such as:

Si cette annee sera abondante ou sterile [Will this year be abundant or sterile?]

Si la femme est enceinte [Is this woman pregnant?]

Si la femme enceinte sera un fils ou une fille [Will a pregnant woman will have a boy or a girl?]

Si les nouvelles sont veritables ou fausses [Is the news true or false?]

Combien de temps tu demeureras encore sans te marier [How many years before you marry?]

Si tu seras heureux en amour [Will you be happy in love?]

Si tu es sage ou non [Are you wise or not]

Si tu mourras pauvre ou riche [Will you die poor or rich?]

But several take on a more serious, or even intrusive, tone, including:

Si l'enfant qui est né est a toy ou a un autre [Is the child yours or someone else's?]

Si le serviteur mourra le premier ou la maistresse [Will the servant or the mistress die first?]

Si la fille est pucelle ou non [Is the girl a virgin or not?]

Si la courtisanne que tu frequentes est dangereuse [Is your mistress dangerous?]

Combien de temps vivront l'homme ou la femme [How long will a man or a woman live?]

Si la femme enceinte accouchera sans danger [Will the pregnant woman give birth safely?]

Each question has a possible 16 answers, listed under a series of headings from astrology or from myth and legend such as *Le taureau* [Taurus], *La vierge* [Virgo], *Les gemeaux* [Gemini], *Mercure* [Mercury], *Achille* [Achilles], *Jason, Merlin,* and *Roland*.

It is in the second part of the work, the *Traité Curieux*, that we get to the subject of symbolism. The volume begins with a long essay on the meanings of different colours as used in heraldry and elsewhere, and this is followed by the floral dictionary. Then comes a section on the significance of different coloured threads to tie a bouquet. This is slightly different from the previous version. It begins by saying:

> *All these plants, flowers, and fruits can be sent on their own, or we can make mysterious bouquets of them, which will symbolise without speaking the loving thoughts of those who send them . . . . If they feel indifference or hatred, or they want to show the anger and contempt they have for someone, they will be able to do it very easily, by presenting them with plants or flowers, whose meanings are unfavourable; or they can even hold this book and laughingly point out such a flower or such a plant to those they want to oblige or disoblige*

*. . . For example, if a damsel does not take pleasure in the
cajoling of someone, and she despises his advances, she can
let him know that his hope is vain by showing him an empty
ear of wheat . . . then, if he continues to importune her too
much, she will show him in the book the deer fern, whose
meaning is you bother me too much, or if she wants to show
him that she does not trust him, it will be good to show him
the apricot blossom whose meaning is I do not trust you. If,
on the other hand, she wishes to favour him with a positive
response, she will show him a white rosebud whose meaning
is I love you, or else she can send him a hairy woodrush which
means you will get what you wish for, and so on.*

The author goes on to point out that the names of flowers can also be
used in letters *"which will appear at first to be full of rigmarole that makes
no sense, but which can be deciphered by the meanings given to each flower
and plant"*. He then gives an example of a proposal of marriage written
with reference to the floral dictionary, before going on to the symbolism
involved in tying a bouquet.

The meanings of the ties are not identical to those published in *La
Recreation, Devis et Mignardise Amoureuse* in 1579. While raw linen
from the spindle, black thread, green thread and red thread keep the same
meanings, there is no longer any mention of greenish blue or grey thread,
or of grass, and no distinction is made between silk and linen thread.
The meanings of the other ties have all been changed to a greater or lesser
extent:

White thread can mean expectation of either a good or bad response,
not just a good response as before.

Hair used to tie a bouquet no longer offers just body, heart and soul to the recipient but also all the worldly goods of the sender. Tan thread is now used to reinforce a negative message.

Yellow thread, while still emphasising the positive meanings of the flowers, also assures the recipient that there is nothing that she can wish for that the sender will not give her.

The meaning for violet thread is now transferred to blue or purple thread, and blue thread loses its previous meaning.

Crimson thread, which previously didn't affect the meanings and indicated that the sender had no expectation of a response, now means that he has hopes of a favourable response, as well as emphasizing the meanings of the flowers.

Gold and silver threads are no longer reserved for the nobility and there is no mention of gold being for men and silver for women. While still reinforcing the positive meanings, they also reduce any negative meanings.

The author finishes by writing about the use of knots in the ends of the threads to indicate that no message is hidden in the flowers *"because it could happen that those who would like to send bouquets would not have silk threads of the colour that would be suitable for their purposes"*

LES RECREATIONS GALANTES 1671

The full title of this volume is: *Les Recreations Galantes contenant diverses questions plaisantes avec leurs reponses. Le passe-temps de plusieurs petits jeux. Quelques enigmes en prose. Le blazon des couleurs sur les livrees et faveurs. L'explication des songes Et un traite de la phisionomie. Suite et seconde partie de la maison des jeux.* It was published in Paris by Estienne Loyson in 1671.

This title translates as:

Genteel recreations containing various delightful questions with their answers. The pastime of several little games. Some riddles in prose. The emblems of colours on liveries and favours. The explanation of dreams. And a treatise on physionomy. A continuation and second part of The House of Games.

The Biblioteque Nationale de France identifies the author of this book as Charles Sorel (c. 1602 –1674) who wrote novels as well as books on science, history and religion. *The House of Games*, of which this is *"a continuation and second part"*, is a compendium of card games.

The book begins with the same fortune-telling question-and-answer game that was in the 1649 volume. There are fewer questions (52 rather than 71) and some of them are new to the list, for example:

Si on recouvera sa debte [Will the person recover the debt?]
Si le secret confié a esté revelé [Has the secret which was confided been revealed]

The lists of answers are now identified just by numbers, not by astrological or legendary names.

Next comes *Les passe-temps des jeux*, a description of 82 different parlour games. After this there are 13 riddles including:

Qui c'etoit qui marchoit sur ses dents? Un horloge. [What walks on its teeth? A clock.]
Qui est un corps sans corps, qui compose les autres corps, et qui n'ayant point de parties, est cause de la production des parties. Un atome. [What is a bodiless body, which makes other bodies, and which having no parts, causes parts to be produced? An atom.]

This is followed by a short treatise on the meanings of colours, the floral dictionary and an essay on the tying of a bouquet with different coloured threads, identical to that in the previous volume.

The next section of the book deals with the interpretation of dreams and the final section is a treatise on physiognomy (reading a person's character from his or her facial characteristics).

THE FLORAL DICTIONARY

It was, perhaps, inevitable that there would be some plants listed that it would be impossible to identify. In the four or five hundred years since these lists were first compiled, not only has the language evolved but names – and, in particular, vernacular names – have changed or have been lost. In addition to which, printing with moveable type was still in its infancy in the 16th and 17th centuries and typographical errors were commonplace. Variations in spelling, too, were the norm. And, of course, it is possible – particularly for the first two volumes – that much, if not all, of the text was being copied from a handwritten original, which would increase the chances of errors still more. That said, it has been possible to identify most of the plants in the dictionary and to make an informed guess as to others. There are, however, a few that – frustratingly – remain unidentified.

When these books were written, the days of the great plant hunters were still in the future, so most of the plants listed would have been native to France or, at least, to other parts of Europe. Where this is not the case, I have mentioned it in the notes.

For each plant, there is a note of which books the meaning appears in. The abbreviations used are:

1/58 (La Recreation et Devis d'Amours 1558)

2/25 (La Recreation Devis et Mignardise Amoureuse 1625)

3/49 (Les Oracles Divertissans & Traite Curieux 1649)

4/71 (Les Recreations Galantes 1671)

I also reference two other editions of *Traite Curieux et Recreatif* and *Oracles Divertissans* which, although almost identical to earlier versions of the dictionary, have slight variations for a few meanings. They were published in 1664 and 1677. If either was the first edition with a particular meaning, these are included and are shown as X1/64 and X2/77.

Variations in the spelling (but not variations in accents) of a plant are noted as 'Var'. The first spelling shown (in upper case bold) is the earliest. For example:

MILLE FUEILLE

Var. Mille feuille

So the format of an entry with two meanings might appear as:

FRENCH PLANT NAME

ENGLISH NAME (Scientific name)

Var. other spellings of plant name

Meaning 1   1/58 • 2/25

Meaning 2   3/49 • 4/71

Notes.

I have shown only the English translations of the meanings unless there is something noteworthy about the French original. This has been done in order to keep the entries as simple as possible, since in many cases a meaning can be expressed in several ways (caused by variations in spelling, vocabulary and phraseology) but all of which translate to the same thing.

When there is 'or' in bold in a meaning, it indicates that both meanings are given in the French – eg 'Esperance incertaine, *ou bien* je ne m'y fie pas' is shown as '**Uncertain hope or I don't trust it**'. However, an '*or*' that is not in bold and is in brackets means that there are two ways in which the French can be translated – eg 'Donnez moy remede' is shown as '**Give me a cure (**or **Give me a solution)**' since 'remede' may be translated as either 'cure' or 'solution'.

While I have given the Latin name of most of the plants to aid identification, it is important to remember that this method of classification only began in the 18th century.

As is common with books of this period, the letter i is often used as a substitute for the letter j, and the letter u for the letter v. To avoid confusion I have 'corrected' these substitutions when they appear in the name of the plant or in any meaning that is quoted.

English plant names prefixed with an asterisk (eg *YARROW) indicate that this is the probable identification, although not 100% certain. Two asterisks (eg **HONEYWORT) means that this is only a possible identification.

Where two English names are separated by commas (eg ALECOST, COSTMARY) it indicates that these are both names given to the same plant. Where the French name can relate to two different plants, these are separated by 'or' (eg BUCKTHORN or BLACKTHORN).

And finally, you may notice that some plants appear in more than one place, with different names and, usually, with different meanings. For example, yarrow is listed as acillets, mille feuille and rejointe. This duplication is not confined to the books covered by this volume – later floral dictionaries sometimes do the same. And it's not just in French that a single plant can have a multitude of names – for example, *Arum maculatum* is known in English as cuckoo pint, lords and ladies, Adam-and-Eve, snakeshead, adder's-root, friar's cowl, starchwort and wake-robin. Of course, this doesn't explain why several meanings should be given to one plant. My own theory is that, since the writers of these floral dictionaries were not botanists, they were working from lists of plants found in other books (these were certainly available in the 16th and 17th centuries) and they didn't appreciate that some plants appeared more than once. Working from a list, rather than from an intimate knowledge of the plants, might also explain why some meanings seem to relate to the appearance or mythology of the plant while others relate only to the name, and still others seem to have no connection between the meaning and the plant itself.

When plants appear more than once under different names, I have put a 'See also' note at the end of the entry. However, in order not to over-complicate matters, I have not put a 'See also' when different parts of one plant follow each other in the listing, eg Abricotier, Abricotier, la fleur d', and Abricot.

I have kept the dictionary in alphabetical order according to the French names of the plants, but you will find an index of English names at the end of the book.

THE
COMBINED
FLORAL
DICTIONARY

ABIOTS

NOT IDENTIFIED

I am chaste and constant   3/49 • 4/71

ABRICOTIER

APRICOT TREE   (Prunus armeniaca)

Disloyalty   3/49 • 4/71

A native of China and Central Asia, the apricot was cultivated as early as 2000 BCE. By 60 BCE it had found its way to Greece and about 100 years later it reached Italy from where it gradually spread through the rest of Europe.

ABRICOTIER, la fleur d'

APRICOT BLOSSOM

I cannot trust you   3/49 • 4/71

ABRICOT

APRICOT

More beautiful than good   3/49 • 4/71

ACHE

CELERY   (Apium graveolens)

Protect me   1/58 • 2/25 • 3/49 •4/71

Wild celery is found growing in marshy ground and, unlike the cultivated variety has an acrid taste and smell. However, the ancient Chinese, Egyptians and Romans all used it medicinally to treat a wide range of complaints – including hangovers.

ACILLETS

*YARROW   (Achillea millefolium)

I will return the favour to you   3/49 • 4/71

See also: MILLE FUEILLE & REJOINTE

The modern French name for yarrow is achillée which is derived from that of Achilles who is said to have used yarrow to heal battle wounds. It is known that, in ancient times, yarrow was used extensively as a healing herb. In the Middle Ages, it was used in Christian exorcism rituals because it was believed both to summon the devil and to expel him. By the start of the 15th century, it was being cultivated in European gardens.

ADIANTOS

MAIDENHAIR FERN   (Adiantum)

Give me a cure (or **Give me a solution**)   3/49 • 4/71

See also: CAPILLI VENERIS

In the 16th century, this small fern was believed to cure a variety of complaints including asthma, cough and snakebites while, in the 17th century, the English herbalist John Gerard wrote "It consumeth and wasteth away the King's Evil and other hard swellings, and it maketh the haire of the head or beard to grow that is fallen and pulled off." It grows mostly where there is plenty of moisture, especially near rocks.

AIGREMOINE

AGRIMONY   (Agrimonia)

Excellent goodness   3/49 • 4/71

Agrimony grows in fields, hedgerows and woodland. In ancient Greece it was used to treat eye problems. The Roman naturalist Pliny recommended it for dysentery and, up to the 16th century, it was also used to treat wounds, gout and rheumatism.

ALLISIER

WILD SERVICE TREE   (Sorbus torminalis)

Drunkenness   3/49 • 4/71

See also: CORMIER

The wild service tree grows in woods and hedges. It produces brown berries that, before the introduction of hops in the Middle Ages, were used to flavour beer. It may be a memory of this that led to the meaning given here.

ALLISIER, le fruit d'

WILD SERVICE TREE FRUIT

You have need of sleep   3/49 • 4/71

ALOYES FLEURIES

*ALOES   (Aloe)

Flower of youth   3/49 • 4/71

The identification of this plant is an informed guess but it seems the most likely candidate. There are over 560 species of flowering succulent plants that fall under the heading of 'aloes'. The best known is Aloe vera which was known to the Chinese and the Sumerians in the third millennium BCE. The ancient Egyptians recognised its anti-inflammatory properties and the physicians of Greece and Rome used it to heal wounds, ulcers and other skin problems, to treat eye conditions and even to prevent hair loss. It is said that Christopher Columbus always took Aloe vera with him on his travels.

ALVISNES

WORMWOOD   (Artemisia absinthium)

Comfort after torment   3/49 • 4/71

Wormwood is a shrub and was known to the Romans as absinthium, meaning 'bitter'. The Greeks used it to treat disorders of the brain and would put the leaves in wine to reduce the intoxicating effect of the alcohol. Wormwood has insecticidal properties and, in the Middle Ages, was strewn around the house to prevent infestations of lice and fleas.

AMANDIER

ALMOND   (Prunus dulcis)

Noise, quarrel, madness and brashness   3/49 • 4/71

The almond tree is native to the Middle East but was being grown in Europe by the mid 16th century.

AMANDIER, la fleur d'

ALMOND BLOSSOM

Uncertain hope or I don't trust it   3/49 • 4/71

AMARANTE

AMARANTH   (Amaranthus caudatus)

I am constant   3/49 • 4/71

See also: PASSE VELOUX & QUEUES DE RENARD

Amaranthus caudatus, also known as love-lies-bleeding, is an annual plant that produces long tails of red flowers. To the Greeks, it symbolised immortality and its name comes from the Greek word 'amaranton' meaning 'everlasting'. It was a popular plant in gardens during the 16th and 17th centuries.

AMAROUFLE

FOETID CHAMOMILE, MAYWEED   (Anthemis cotula)

Give me leave   3/49 • 4/71

Foetid chamomile (also known as stinking chamomile) grows in cornfields and on waste ground and was used medicinally in the Middle Ages.

ANCOLIE

COLUMBINE   (Aquilegia vulgaris)

Don't be sad   3/49 • 4/71

See also: ENCOLIE

A hardy perennial, A. vulgaris has violet-blue, pink or white flowers and is found growing wild in meadows and thickets.

ANIS

ANISEED   (Pimpinella anisum)

Var: Avis (probably a misprint)

Comfort   1/58 • 2/25

Comfort yourself or Comfort me   3/49 • 4/71

Native to the Mediterranean region, aniseed was used in the ancient world for flavouring and as a medicine and an aphrodisiac. It has feathery leaves and dense flat-topped clusters of white or yellow flowers.

APARITOIRE

PELLITORY   (Parietaria officinalis)

Free will   3/49 • 4/71

A non-stinging perennial plant of the nettle family, pellitory is often found growing on walls. Its name is derived from the Latin 'herba parietaria' meaning 'plant of walls'.

ARGENTINE

SILVERWEED   (Potentilla anserine)

or SNOW IN SUMMER   (Cerastium tomentosum)

Let's not talk about it any more   1/58 • 2/25 • 3/49 • 4/71

Argentine is the name given to both silverweed and snow in summer. The first of these has long, creeping stems with yellow five-petalled flowers and leaves whose underside is silvery in colour. It appears regularly in mediaeval herbals and was used to treat diarrhoea and haemorrhages. It tends to grow by rivers, in meadows and by the roadside. Snow in summer is a low-growing, spreading perennial with silvery-grey, narrow leaves and star-shaped white flowers.

ARMOISIE

MUGWORT   (Artemisia vulgaris)

I honour you   3/49 • 4/71

See also: HERBE S. JEAN

Mugwort has been grown in gardens since Roman times. It has been made into love potions and medicines, and has been used to kill insects and to flavour food.

ARODE

ORACHE, MOUNTAIN SPINACH   (Atriplex)

I don't care about you   3/49 • 4/71

Orache has been eaten as a vegetable since prehistoric times and is even mentioned in the Book of Job in the Old Testament as a food eaten by outcasts. There are many species, all of which tend to grow in salty soil, resulting in the leaves having a salty flavour.

ARTICHAUT

GLOBE ARTICHOKE   (Cynara cardunculus var. scolymus)

Your business is dangerous   3/49 • 4/71

Native to the Mediterranean region, the artichoke is actually a species of thistle. It was eaten as a vegetable by the ancient Greeks and Romans but then fell out of favour for a millennium or more. It started to regain its popularity in 15th century Italy and, a century later, was being eaten throughout France.

ASPERGES

ASPARAGUS   (Asparagus officinalis)

Honest conversion   3/49 • 4/71

X1/64 and X2/77 change 'honneste conventure' to 'honneste couverture' which means 'good coverage'. This may, however, just be a misprint.

Asparagus was eaten by the ancient Greeks and Romans, the former believing it to be an aphrodisiac. Like the artichoke, asparagus fell out of favour as a vegetable for many years but, by the 16th century, was being enjoyed by the aristocracy of Europe – Louis XIV of France (1638-1715) is said to have been very fond of it. The inclusion of such an exclusive – and, no doubt, expensive – vegetable in these early floral dictionaries suggests that the people who bought the books would have been people of high status.

ASPIC

SPIKE LAVENDER   (Lavandula latifolia)

Better yourself   1/58 • 2/25 • 3/49 • 4/71

See also: LAVANDE

Differing slightly in shape and smell from English lavender (Lavendula angustifolia), Lavandula latifolia is native to the western Mediterranean region and was spread across Europe by the Romans. It has been grown in gardens since ancient times.

ASPIC, feuille d'

LEAF OF SPIKE LAVENDER

You control me too much   3/49 • 4/71

AUBESPINE FLEURIE

HAWTHORN   (Crataegus oxyacantha)

Kiss me   3/49 • 4/71

See also: ESPINE BLANCHE

Found in hedges, thickets and copses, the hawthorn is native to Europe. The wood, which is hard and strong, has been used by turners and millwrights, while the roots have been used by cabinet makers.

AUREOLLE

SPURGE LAUREL   Daphne laureola)

It will never happen to me   1/58 • 3/49 • 4/71

See also: LAUREOLLE

Neither a spurge nor a laurel, despite its name, this bushy evergreen shrub has dark green shiny leaves and greenish yellow flowers.

AVOINE

OATS   (Avena sativa)

Var: Avione (probably a misprint)

I want to chastise you   3/49 • 4/71

See also: ESPY D'AVOINE

Wild oats growing in the Middle East were used for food over 30,000 years ago and, by Roman times, the cultivated variety was established in Europe.

BASELIC

BASIL   (Ocimum basilicum)

Var: Basselic

Regret   1/58 • 2/25

I have great regret   3/49 • 4/71

Originating in tropical Asia and Africa, basil is known to have been grown by the ancient Greeks who, believing it would ward off evil spirits, used it in funeral ceremonies.

BASSINETZ

DOUBLE YELLOW VIOLET

Var: Violette jaune double qu'autrement l'on appelle bassinets [double yellow violets, otherwise known as bassinets]

Be satisfied   1/58 • 2/25

Perfect beauty   3/49 • 4/71

See also all entries under VIOLETTE

BAUSME

COMMON BALM   (Melissa officinalis)

You are too quick to believe   3/49 • 4/71

See also: PIMANT

Native to southern Europe, balm's attractiveness to bees was understood by the ancient Greeks who put sprigs of it in hives to attract swarms. Used by the ancients as a treatment for hypochondria, it was described by the 11th century Persian physician Avicenna as causing the mind and heart to become merry. Cultivated since the 16th century, or earlier, it is also known as lemon balm because of its lemon-scented leaves.

BETOYNE
> BETONY   (Stachys officinalis)
> Var: Bettoine
> **Resistance**   1/58 • 2/25 • 3/49 • 4/71
> Found in woods, on heaths and in pastures, betony was used medicinally by the ancients. The 2nd century Roman philosopher Apuleius wrote that it benefitted both soul and body, and protected against visions and dreams. The plant has also been used to make a dark yellow dye for wool.

BETTE BLANCHE
> WHITE CHARD   (Beta vulgaris)
> **Time is wasted** (or **Time is wasting**)   3/49 • 4/71
> Also known as Swiss chard, this green leafy plant, which originated from a wild beet native to southern Europe, has been eaten as a vegetable for over 1000 years.

BETTE ROUGE
> *BEETROOT
> **Don't think about it anymore**   3/49 • 4/71
> The roots of beets were first cultivated as a vegetable in the 16th

century, probably in Italy or Germany.

BLEUVETTE PERCE

CORNFLOWER, BACHELOR'S BUTTON   (Centaurea cyanus)

Var: Bluette perse

I like your vivacity (or **I like your wit**)   1/58 • 3/49 • 4/71

The cornflower, which is native to south east Europe, was popular in 16th century gardens. Wild varieties can be dark blue, white or violet, while cultivated red and pink versions had been developed by the early 17th century.

BLEUVETTE VIOLETTE

VIOLET CORNFLOWER

Var: Bluette violette

You are my satisfaction   1/58 • 2/25 • 3/49

You are all my satisfaction   X1/64 • 4/71

BOUILLON

MULLEIN   (Verbascum thapsus)

Initial pain   3/49 • 4/71

See also: MOLAINE & VERMINEUSE

Mullein produces dense spikes of yellow flowers which Roman women soaked in lye to make a bleach for their hair. Pliny, the Roman naturalist, wrote that figs would not go rotten if they were wrapped in mullein leaves. In the Middle Ages, mullein was believed to protect against demons. And an infusion of the flowers was popular in France as a cough remedy.

BOURACHE

BORAGE   (Borrago officinalis)

Var: Bourrache

Reproach   1/58 • 2/25

I blame you   3/49 • 4/71

Borage can be found growing on waste land, rubbish dumps and roadsides. A native of southern Europe, it produces clusters of bright blue flowers.

BOURDAINE

ALDER BUCKTHORN   (Frangula alnus)

I'm waiting for help   1/58 • 3/49 • 4/71

Growing in woods and thickets, the flowers of the alder buckthorn are particularly attractive to bees. In the autumn it produces dark purple or black berries. The bark can be used to make a yellow dye, while charcoal derived from the wood was favoured by manufacturers of gunpowder.

BOURDON DE GIRON

*SPIDER ORCHID   (Ophrys frelon)

I offer you my service   1/58 • 3/49 • 4/71

I found two possibilities for this plant. The spider orchid, Ophrys frelon, is known as bourdon, while one of the names of the hollyhock is bourdon de S. Jacques. However, the word 'giron' denotes a triangular shape in heraldry and this is a shape that seems to fit the orchid rather better than the hollyhock. The spider orchid likes limestone soils and grows in meadows, on hillsides and along the edges of roads and fields.

BOURSE À EVESQUE

NOT IDENTIFIED

Make a sudden response   3/49 • 4/71

BROME

BROME   (Bromus)

I am waiting for you   1/58

Brome is the name given to a large genus of grasses, growing in many different habitats throughout the temperate regions of the world.

BRUERE

HEATHER, LING   (Calluna vulgaris and species of Erica)

Var: Bruyere, Bruyeres

Harshness (or Rudeness)   1/58 • 2/25 • 3/49 • 4/71

Heather is the name commonly given to both Calluna and Erica (although, strictly speaking, the correct name for Erica is 'heath').

BRUNETTE

SELF-HEAL, HEAL-ALL   (Prunella vulgaris)

Var: Bruvette (probably a misprint)

Receive me   3/49 • 4/71

The plant, which has violet-blue clusters of flowers, used to be used medicinally in Germany to treat conditions of the jaws and throat.

BUGLOSSE

ALKANET, COMMON BUGLOSS   (Anchusa officinalis)

Var: Buglose

Lightness   1/58 • 2/25 • 3/49 • 4/71

The name 'bugloss' is derived from the Greek 'bous glossa' meaning ox tongue, referring to the shape and roughness of the leaves. The plant has purple flowers, similar to those of forget-me-nots, and tends to grow on waste land and at the sides of roads and fields.

BUIS

BOX   (Buxus sempervirens)

Var: Bouis

Rejoicing   1/58 • 3/49 • 4/71

Joy, mirth   2/25

An evergreen shrub or small tree with glossy, dark green leaves, box is native to western and southern Europe.

CAMOMILLE

CHAMOMILE   (Matricaria chamomilla)

I shall always support you   3/49 • 4/71

The plant name derives from the Greek 'chamo melo' meaning 'fallen apple' and relates to its scent. It has feathery leaves and white daisy-like flowers and has been grown in gardens since ancient times. Its use as a medication dates back to the 13th century or earlier.

CANNES

REED   (Phragmites australis or Arundo donax)

Labours   3/49 • 4/71

See also: ROSEAU

The term 'reed' is used to describe a number of tall grass-like plants that grow in wet soil. Probably the best known of these are the common reed (Phragmites australis) and the giant reed (Arundo donax). The common reed has been used over many centuries to thatch roofs, while the giant reed, used by the ancient Greeks to make flutes, is still used to make reeds for woodwind instruments. The giant reed, which is native to the Middle East, will grow next to fresh or salt water and can reach up to 30 feet in height. The common reed, which is native to Europe, is considerably smaller and grows mostly in fresh water to a height of about 9 feet.

CAPILLI VENERIS

MAIDENHAIR FERN   (Adiantum capillus veneris)
Humility   1/58 • 3/49 • 4/71
See also: ADIANTOS

CARCHANGES

CHINESE LANTERN   (Physalis alkekengi)
Happiness   3/49 • 4/71
A garden plant since Roman times, the Chinese lantern (also known as winter cherry) is native to southern Europe, growing on exposed areas of hills. It produces yellow bell-shaped flowers, after which the sepals develop into dark orange 'lanterns' enclosing red berries.

CEDRE

CEDAR   (Larix cedrus)
Excellence (or **Height**)   3/49 • 4/71
Native to Asia Minor, the cedar is believed to have provided the wood used to build Solomon's temple. An evergreen conifer, it has been known in Europe from the 13th century and can grow to a height of over 100 feet.

CERESIER

CHERRY TREE   (Prunus avium)
Var: Cerisier
Don't forget me   1/58 • 2/25 • 3/49 • 4/71
The cultivated cherry was brought from Asia to Italy in 73 CE by the

Roman general Lucullus. Its Latin name (cerasus) is that of the town in which he found it. Its wood is hard and tough and has, over the years, been used by cabinet makers, turners and makers of musical instruments. Fredrik Hasselqvist (1722-1752), a Swedish naturalist and traveller, is quoted (in a number of sources from the 18th and 19th centuries) as having said that, during a siege, over 100 men stayed alive for nearly two months with nothing to eat other than the gum that cherry trees exude when their bark is damaged. The location and date of this siege are not stated and, as far as I know, there is no record of when or where Hasselqvist said or wrote this, so it may just be an early example of an urban legend.

CERFUEIL

CHERVIL   (Anthriscus cerefolium)

Var: Cerfeuil

Virtue by all   1/58 • 2/25 • 3/49 • 4/71

This herb is related to parsley and is native to the Caucasus (the region between the Black Sea and the Caspian Sea). It was spread throughout Europe by the Romans. Its name derives from the Greek 'charas phylla' meaning 'leaves of joy'

CETERAC

SCALY SPLEENWORT, SCALE FERN (Ceterach officinarum)

Allegiance   3/49 • 4/71

Unusually for a fern, scaly spleenwort will grow in full sun and doesn't need much in the way of humidity.

CHANGRE ou HERBE ROBERT

HERB ROBERT   (Geranium robertianum)

Don't think I'm like this   3/49 • 4/71

I have been unable to identify 'changre'. I think, therefore, that it is best to assume that both names refer to the same plant, with 'changre' being a vernacular name, albeit unrecorded, for Herb Robert. A species of cranesbill with pink flowers and an unpleasant smell, it grows on waste ground, on walls and grassy banks and under hedges. It is named – although I have been unable to find out why – after St. Robert of Molesme (1028-1111), one of the founders of the Cistercian Order.

CHANGRE AZURÉE, fleur de

AZURE CRANESBILL FLOWER

Remember me   3/49 • 4/71

Since the flowers of herb Robert are pink, it seems fair to assume that 'changre azurée' refers to a blue cranesbill.

CHANGRE ROUGE, fleur de

RED CRANESBILL FLOWER

Be joyful   3/49 • 4/71

CHANVRE

CANNABIS   (Cannabis sativa)

Defiance (or **Distrust**)   1/58 • 2/25

Native to Asia, this plant arrived in Europe well over 1000 years ago. Over the years it has been used to make a strong fibre (hemp) for ropes and sacking, and to provide medicine. The Romans used it to treat earache, gout and arthritis, and to reduce sexual desire, and its mood enhancing properties have probably been known for several millennia.

CHARDON

THISTLE   (Carduus)

I want you badly   1/58 • 2/25

Sweetness is within   3/49 • 4/71

This may relate to any one of a number of species of thistle. Those native to Europe include C. acanthoides and C. pycnocephalus. The former can grow to 6 feet or more, the latter is somewhat smaller.

CHARDON BENIST

BLESSED, or HOLY, THISTLE HERB (Cnicus benedictus)

The thought (or **dream**) **of your advancement**   1/58

Native to the Mediterranean region, this yellow-flowered thistle was once thought to have supernatural healing powers.

CHASTAIGNE & son herisson

CHESTNUT TREE AND ITS NUT   (Castanea sativa)

I'm not afraid of you   3/49 • 4/71

Don't be afraid   X2/77

This probably refers to the sweet chestnut, which is a European native, rather than the horse chestnut which was only introduced into Europe from Asia in the mid 16th century. 'Herisson' translates literally as 'hedgehog' and it is easy to see why this should be a vernacular term for the spiky case of the nut. The name 'chastaigne' derives from Castonis – the name of a town in Greece where chestnuts were grown. The wood of the chestnut tree is similar to oak, but more lightweight, and over the years has been used for cabinet making, carpentry and joinery. The trees, if left undisturbed, can live to around 600 years or even more.

CHASTAIGNER, fueille de
CHESTNUT LEAF
Var: Chastaigner et sa feüille
Advise me   1/58 • 2/25 • 3/49 • 4/71

CHESNE
OAK   (Quercus robur)
Safety   1/58 • 2/25
Be safe and fear nothing   3/49 • 4/71
Fossil records show that trees similar to the oak first appeared around 35 million years ago. Trees that would probably be recognisable today as oaks appeared about 23 million years ago. The oak is native to the northern hemisphere, and there are numerous species.

CHESNE, gomme de
OAK TREE RESIN
Don't trust it   3/49 • 4/71

CHEVRE-FEUIL
HONEYSUCKLE   (Lonicera caprifolium)
Loyal acquaintance   3/49 • 4/71
See also: PENTECOUSTE
A native of central and southern Europe, wild honeysuckle grows in woods, hedges and thickets. A vigorous climber, it is known for its profusion of sweetly scented flowers.

CHIEN-DENT
COUCHGRASS   (Elymus repens)
Advice   3/49 • 4/71

A fast-growing perennial grass, couchgrass can grow to 4 feet high and is native to most of Europe.

CHOU, la feuille

CABBAGE LEAF   (Brassica oleracea)

Providence   3/49 • 4/71

The cabbage, of which there are numerous species, has been cultivated for many centuries and was a favourite vegetable of the Romans.

CHOU, la fleur

CAULIFLOWER   (Brassica oleracea var. botrytis)

New worry   3/49 • 4/71

Two mediaeval Arabian botanists believed that the cauliflower originated in Cyprus. It was brought from Italy to France in the early 16th century. Nowadays its French name is just one word – choufleur - but a French-English dictionary of 1611 lists it as 'chou fleur', 'chou fleuris' or 'chou floris' and its English translation as 'collyflorie'.

CICADO

NOT IDENTIFIED

Var: Cicad, Cicados

Lasting love   1/58 • 2/25 • 3/49 • 4/71

CICATOLIC

NOT IDENTIFIED

Wealth   3/49 • 4/71

CICORÉE

CHICORY   (Cichorium intybus)

Good address and good grace   3/49 • 4/71

See also: SCARIOLLE OU CICORÉE

Chicory is native to most of Europe. The ancient Greeks called it kichora.

CIVE

CHIVES   (Allium schoenoprasum)

From bad to worse   3/49 • 4/71

Used in cookery from the 14th century or earlier, the name derives from the Latin word for onion. Chives produce dense button-like bunches of flowers in pink, purple or white.

COCHET

GOAT'S BEARD   (Tragopogon pratensis)

Mockery   3/49 • 4/71

Found growing in fields and along the side of roads, goat's beard looks rather like a dandelion, with yellow flowers and large fluffy seed-heads. However, unlike the dandelion, the flowers only open for a few hours a day and close around noon.

COIGNER

QUINCE   (Cydonia oblonga)

I want it very much   3/49 • 4/71

The quince is native to central Asia but many varieties were known to Pliny the Elder in the first century CE. The tree produces bright golden-yellow fruits that look somewhat like pears although they can grow much larger.

COQ

ALECOST, COSTMARY   (Tanacetum balsamita)

Var: Cocq

I ask (or beg) you to be my wife   1/58 • 2/25 • 3/49 • 4/71

I found several candidates for 'coq' but most sources pointed me towards 'coq des jardins' and 'menthe coq', both of which are names for alecost. Native to western Asia, it was brought to Europe around the 15th century. It has yellow button-like flowers, and its mint-scented leaves were used in the past to flavour ale.

CORIANDE

CORIANDER   (Coriandrum sativum)

You (f) stink   [vous estes punaise]   3/49

You (m) stink   [vous estes punais]   4/71

You are sorry   [vous estes penaise]   X1/64

The first meaning probably derives from the plant name itself, since 'coriander' comes from the Greek word 'koris' meaning 'a bug' and relates to the unpleasant smell of the leaves. The variation in meanings, however, is interesting. 3/49's 'vous estes punaise', tells us that the person being spoken to is female. 4/71, however, turns the recipient into a male by dropping the 'e' off the end of 'punais'. Whether the author of X1/64 decided that, perhaps it was unkind to tell people they stank, or whether the change was just a misprint – an 'e' replacing the 'u' to make 'vous estes penaise' – it is impossible to say.

CORMIER

SERVICE TREE   (Sorbus domestica)

Var: Cermier

I languish in anguish   1/58 • 2/25 • 3/49 • 4/71

See also: ALLISIER

A deciduous tree that is native to the mountains of Europe, the service tree's wood is very hard and has been used over the centuries for making measuring sticks of all kinds.

CORNE DE CERF

SWINE CRESS   (Lepidium coronopus)

3/49 • 4/71

The meaning is not clear. The French is 'à vostre dam', which may mean 'to your loss' or it may be a form of address, since a 1611 French-English dictionary gives the additional meaning of 'dam' as 'a title of respect and honour given in courtesie unto a Gentleman or Knight'.

Swine cress (also known as creeping wart cress) is a member of the mustard family and is native to Europe. It grows on waste ground, in fields or on shingle. The French name translates literally to 'stag's horn'.

CORNEILLIER

DOGWOOD   (Cornus sanguinea)

Despite you   3/49 • 4/71

A native of Europe, dogwood has been put to many uses. Its twigs were used in the past to make baskets, its black berries to make ink and, in Roman times, the wood was used to make weapons.

COULDRE

HAZEL OR HAZELNUTS   (Corylus avellana)

Var: Coudres des noisillier

Trust me   [tenez moy foy]   1/58 • 2/25

Hold me tight   [tenez moy fort]   3/49 • 4/71

See also: NOISILLIER

Here again, a change in just one letter changes the entire meaning but it's impossible to say whether or not it was done deliberately. The hazel grows in the temperate regions of the northern hemisphere and produces pale yellow catkins before the leaves come out in the spring.

COURONNE IMPERIALLE

CROWN IMPERIAL   (Fritillaria imperialis)

I shall serve you   3/49 • 4/71

This species of fritillary came from Turkey, where it had long been a favourite in gardens, and was introduced to western Europe towards the end of the 16th century.

CRESSON D'EAU

WATERCRESS   (Nasturtium officinale)

Foresight   3/49 • 4/71

Watercress was well known in the ancient world. The soldiers of King Xerxes' army (5th century BCE) were ordered to eat it to keep them healthy and free from scurvy. In the same century the Greek physician Hippocrates built his first hospital next to a stream so he had a supply of watercress for his patients.

CRESSON DE JARDIN

*GARDEN CRESS   (Lepidium sativum)

Solace and comfort   3/49 • 4/71

This is one of the more ancient salad plants and probably came originally from western Asia.

CUYRAGE

RED SHANK, PERSICARIA   (Persicaria maculosa)

Var: Cuyrasse, Cuirage

You serve me badly   1/58 • 2/25 • 3/49 • 4/71

An annual herb that grows to about 3 feet tall, persicaria produces dense spikes of pink flowers.

CYTREULLE

PUMPKIN   (Cucurbita maxima)

Var: Citrouille

I say goodbye to you   1/58

We say goodbye   3/49 • 4/71

See also: POTIRON

Pumpkins are native to Mexico and the southern United States, where they have been cultivated for millennia. They were introduced into Europe in the late 15th century.

DENT DE LION, fleur de

DANDELION FLOWER   (Taraxacum)

Var: Dent de lyon

You are wasting time   1/58 • 2/25 • 3/49 • 4/71

You will waste time   X1/64

In the 16th century a decoction of the whole plant was believed to be an effective treatment for jaundice. The juice of the plant has also been used to treat eczema and other skin complaints. A vernacular French name for it is pissenlit ('wet the bed') based on the popular belief that picking the flowers will cause night-time 'accidents'. In fact, the dandelion is a diuretic – but it has to be eaten, not just picked!

DOUVES AQUATIQUES

*WATER CROWFOOT   (Ranunculus aquatilis)

Unhappy acquaintance   3/49 • 4/71

I could not find any reference to 'douves aquatiques' but 'herbe aux douves' is another name for Ranunculus bulbosus (the buttercup), so Ranunculus aquatilis (the water crowfoot) seemed a likely candidate. Water crowfoot is found in stagnant water and has fan-shaped leaves that lie both on and under the water. The flowers are white and can be very large.

EAULNE

ELECAMPANE   (Inula helenium)

Var: Eaume, Enula campana

Certain help (or **Certain relief**)   1/58 • 2/25 • 3/49 • 4/71

There are many species of elecampane, which has large yellow flowers that look like double sunflowers. It can grow to over 6 feet tall, with leaves up to 30 inches long. it was used medicinally by the ancient Greeks.

ELLEBORE

HELLEBORE   (Helleborus)

Think about danger   3/49 • 4/71

See also: PATTE D'OURS

There are a number of species of hellebore including H. foetidus (stinking hellebore), H. niger (black hellebore) and H. viridis (green hellebore). The last two are also known as Christmas rose. H. foetidus is an evergreen with drooping clusters of yellow-green flowers edged with purple; the leaves, if bruised, give off a very unpleasant smell. H. niger has single white flowers, up to 4 inches across, while H. viridis has drooping clusters of green cup-shaped flowers. All hellebores are poisonous.

ENCOLIE

COLUMBINE   (Aquilegia)

Don't take too much   1/58 • 3/49 • 4/71

See also: ANCOLIE

ENDINE

*ENDIVE   (Cichorium endivia)

When you wish   3/49 • 4/71

I have been unable to find 'endine' as the name of a plant and suspect that this is a misprint that was uncorrected when copied into the later volume. Endive is thought to be native to Egypt and to southern Asia but has been cultivated in Europe since the 16th century. There are two types – curly endive and the less bitter broad-leaved endive.

EPEURGE

CAPER SPURGE, GOPHERPLANT   (Euphorbia lathyris)

Var: Espur, Espurge

One more time   1/58 • 2/25 • 3/49 • 4/71

The seeds of caper spurge have, in the past, been used as a substitute for capers (hence the English name) even though they are potentially poisonous.

ERABLE

ACER, MAPLE   (Acer)

Powerlessness   3/49 • 4/71

See also: SICOMORRE

There are many species of Acer, mostly native to Asia and North America. Some however, are European, such as the sycamore (A. pseudoplatanus), the hedge or field maple (Acer campestre), the Norway maple (Acer platanoides) and the Italian maple (Acer opalus). Most have palmate leaves (resembling a hand) which turn bright yellow, orange or red in the autumn.

ESCHERVIS

SKIRRET   (Sium sisarum)

Delicacy (or Confection)   1/58 • 2/25 • 3/49 • 4/71

Although native to China, skirret had arrived in Europe by Roman times. Grown as a root vegetable, it was described by the English agriculturalist John Worlidge (1640–1700) as "the sweetest, whitest and most pleasant of roots".

ESCLERE ou CELIDOINE

GREATER CELANDINE   (Chelidonium majus)

Be more careful   3/49 • 4/71

The plant name comes from the Greek 'chelidon' meaning a swallow, since it is said to start flowering when the swallows arrive and finish flowering when they leave. It can be found in shady places by the side of walls and hedges, and produces yellow flowers, which can be up to an inch across.

ESCLOPPE CHIEN

PETTY WHIN, NEEDLE FURZE   (Genista anglica)

Don't rush   3/49 • 4/71

A small spiny shrub with yellow flowers, petty whin grows on wet heathland and on the edges of bogs.

ESGLANTIER

DOG ROSE, BRIAR ROSE, WILD ROSE   (Rosa canina)

Friendship   1/58 • 2/25

Perfect love   3/49 • 4/71

This probably refers to the whole plant rather than just the flower which has a separate entry (see below). Found in hedges, woods and thickets, the five-petalled flowers of the dog rose can be up to two and a half inches across and any shade from white to deep pink.

ESGLANTIER, rose d'

DOG ROSE FLOWER

I love you above all   3/49 • 4/71

ESPERVANCHE

PERIWINKLE   (Vinca major & minor)

Var: Espervenche, Espervance, Espervane

Experience   1/58 • 2/25 • 3/49 • 4/71

The periwinkle can be a shrub or a herbaceous perennial. It has dark green leaves and purple star-shaped flowers and tends to grow under trees and bushes.

ESPINARS

SPINACH   (Spinacia oleracea)

I can't without you   3/49 • 4/71

Thought to have come originally from Persia and spread, in the 7th century, to India and China, spinach was being grown in the Mediterranean region by the 10th century, arriving in Spain by the end of the 12th century and in France in the 14th. It became popular because it was ready to eat in early spring, before any other fresh vegetables

ESPINE

A THORN

Danger   1/58 • 2/25 • 3/49 • 4/71

ESPINE BLANCHE

HAWTHORN   (Crataegus oxyacantha)

See also: AUBESPINE FLEURIE

Happy reward for prolonged work   3/49 • 4/71

ESPINE BLANCHE FLEURIE

FLOWERING HAWTHORN

Kiss me   3/49 • 4/71

ESPINE NOIRE FLEURIE

BUCKTHORN   (Rhamnus catharticus)

or BLACKTHORN   (Prunus spinosa)

Honourable research   3/49 • 4/71

This may refer to the common buckthorn (Rhamnus catharticus) or the blackthorn (Prunus spinosa), otherwise known as the sloe. Both can take the form of shrubs or small trees. R. catharticus has glossy dark green leaves and tiny yellow-green flowers. The unripe yellow berries have been used to colour paper, and a yellow dye can also be made from the bark. Prunus spinosa has larger five-petalled white flowers that come out just before the leaves.

ESPY DE BLED

EAR OF WHEAT   (Triticum aestivum)

Seek for goodness and riches   3/49 • 4/71

See also: ESPY DE FROMENT

Wheat was being cultivated in Turkey by about 10,000 BCE, in Greece, Cyprus and Egypt by 6000 BCE and in Germany and Spain by 5000 BCE.

ESPI DE BLED CHARGÉ

FULL EAR OF WHEAT

Var: Espic de bled chargé

You will have riches   1/58

It will be well for you   2/25

ESPI DE BLED VUIDE

EMPTY EAR OF WHEAT

Var: Espy de bled vuide

Vain hope   1/58 • 3/49 • 4/71

ESPY DE BLED DOUBLE

TWO EARS OF WHEAT

Hope and contentment   3/49 • 4/71

ESPY DE BLED TRIPLE

THREE EARS OF WHEAT

Certain wealth   3/49 • 4/71

ESPY DE FROMENT

EAR OF WHEAT

Fair rent and legitimately acquired property   3/49 • 4/71

See also: ESPY DE BLED

ESPY D'AVOINE

EAR OF OATS

Take care   3/49 • 4/71

SEE ALSO: AVOINE

ESPY D'ORGE

EAR OF BARLEY   (Hordeum vulgare)

Pain and profit   3/49 • 4/71

Barley was being cultivated by 5000 BCE in Egypt and by 3000 BCE in Europe. It was the main source of bread flour for the ancient Hebrews, Greeks and Romans and for much of Europe until the 16th century.

ESTOURNELLE

NOT IDENTIFIED

Forgive me   3/49 • 4/71

FEBUE, FEÜILLE DE
BEAN LEAF

Avarice   3/49 • 4/71

Oddly enough, this entry probably doesn't refer to what we nowadays call French beans (Phaseolus vulgaris), since these originated in south and central America. Although they and other types of bean were brought to Europe in the 16th century, other 'beans' such as broad beans and chickpeas were far more familiar at the time, having been grown in Europe for centuries. Broad beans originated in the Himalayan foothills, were buried with the dead in ancient Egypt and are mentioned (with chickpeas) in Homer's Iliad (written in the 8th century BCE).

FEBUE, fleur de
BEAN FLOWER

I'm all yours   3/49 • 4/71

FEBUE, la gousse de
BEAN POD

Look after me well   3/49 • 4/71

FEUES, fleur de

BEAN FLOWER

Benign and human appeal   1/58

Benign and human attractions   2/25

FENOIL

FENNEL   (Foeniculum vulgare)

Var: Fenoüil

Pretence (or **Deceit**)   1/58 • 2/25 • 3/49 • 4/71

A strong-smelling perennial plant with dark green feathery leaves and flat-topped clusters of yellow flowers, fennel was used both as a vegetable and in medications by the ancient Egyptians, Greeks and Romans. Roman soldiers believed that eating the seeds would give them strength and courage, while Greek athletes believed it would help them to control their weight. In the Middle Ages, fennel was thought to be a protection against evil.

FIGUIER

FIG TREE   (Ficus carica)

Pangs of conscience   1/58 • 2/25 • 3/49 • 4/71

The common fig is a large shrub or small spreading tree, often grown against walls. Native to the Mediterranean region, it has been grown for its fruit since ancient times.

FIGUES

FIG

Profitable youth   3/49 • 4/71

FLAMBE ou IRIS, fleur de

BEARDED IRIS   (Iris × germanica)

Var: Yris ou flambe, Yris ou flamble

Disappointing attraction   1/58

I don't want to see you   3/49 • 4/71

The bearded (or German) iris is a native of southern Europe. Its root has been used in the past in medications and as a beauty treatment to remove freckles.

FOINE ou GRAINE DE FOUSTEAU

BEECH NUTS   (Fagus silvatica)

You are not without treachery   3/49 • 4/71

See also: FOUTEAU

The beech tree can grow to a height of over 120 feet and is found in forests in the temperate parts of Europe. Its wood is used to make furniture, floors, staircases and musical instruments.

FOUGERE

BRACKEN, FERN   (Pteridium or Osmunda)

Suffering   1/58 • 2/25 • 3/49 • 4/71

See also: ADIANTOS, CAPILLI VENERIS, CETERAC, FOUGEROLLE, POLLIPODE & SCALOPENDRE

There are many species of fern native to Europe, varying in height from about 12 inches to 6 feet.

FOUGEROLLE

DEER FERN   (Blechnum spicant)

You bother me too much   3/49 • 4/71

This is an evergreen fern that grows in woodlands and on heathland

and moors. It can grow to 2 feet tall and 3 feet wide

.

FOUTEAU

BEECH TREE   (Fagus silvatica)

Var: Fousteau,Forsteau

Fake love   1/58 • 3/49 • 4/71

See also: FOINE

FRAISE ou la fleur

STRAWBERRY OR ITS FLOWER   (Fragaria)

Amiable and agreeable gentleness   [Aimable et agreable douceur]   3/49 • 4/71

An easy gait and agreeable gentleness   [Amble et agreable douceur] – probably a misprint   X1/64

The Romans used the wild strawberry medicinally, as did monks in mediaeval Europe. But although wild strawberries were being transplanted into gardens by the 14th century, it was probably another century before attempts were made to cultivate them.

FRAISIER, la feüille de

STRAWBERRY LEAF

Pain without profit   3/49 • 4/71

FRANBOYSE

RASPBERRY   (Rubus idaeus)

Var: Flamboise, Framboisier

Misfortune   1/58 • 2/25 • 3/49 • 4/71

Probably originating in Asia Minor, raspberries were spread through Europe by the Romans. A 4th century book on agriculture, Opus agriculturae, by the Roman writer Palladius mentions the cultivation of raspberries. In the Middle Ages, wild raspberries were used medicinally – and their juice was used to make a red ink.

FRESGON

BOX-HOLLY   (Ruscus aculeatus)

You are too quarrelsome   3/49 • 4/71

Box-holly is a small, slow-growing evergreen shrub that rarely grows to more than 3 feet either in height or width. It has dark green leaves and small light green flowers which are followed by bright red, shiny berries.

FRESGON, la greine de

BOX-HOLLY BERRY

You have neither faith nor law (or **authority**)   3/49 • 4/71

FRESNE

ASH TREE   (Fraxinus excelsior)

Obedience and subjection   3/49 • 4/71

The wood of the ash tree has long been valued for its hardness and resilience. In ancient times it was used to make the shafts of spears; later it was used by wheelwrights, cartwrights and coachmakers and also for building and to make a variety of objects such as ploughs, ladders and oars.

FUMETERRE

FUMITORY   (Fumaria officinalis)

Withdraw   1/58 • 2/25 • 3/49 • 4/71

The name comes from the Latin 'fumus' meaning 'smoke' and alludes to the smell the plant exudes. It has red, tubular flowers and can be found in fields and in the fissures of rocks, growing to a height of about 12 inches.

GALIOT

WOOD AVENS, HERB-BENNET   (Geum urbanum)

When you wish   3/49 • 4/71

Found in woods and hedges, wood avens is a straggly plant that grows to about 2 feet tall and has yellow flowers.

GANTELÉE

FOXGLOVE   (Digitalis purpurea)

You bring me misfortune and great pain   3/49 • 4/71

Used for centuries as a herbal remedy to treat a wide range of complaints including abscesses, headaches, epilepsy and dropsy (congestive heart failure), the foxglove was not cultivated as a garden flower until the 15th century. It is a natural source of digoxin which, nowadays, is manufactured synthetically to treat heart conditions.

GANTELLEE ou FLOQUEZ, fleur de

FOXGLOVE FLOWER

Var: La fleur de gantelée appellée floquets, Fleur de gatellee ou floquez

Tell me what you want   1/58 • 2/25 • 3/49

Tell me your wish   X1/64 • 4/71

GENEST

BROOM   (Genista)

Address   1/58 • 3/49 • 4/71

This shrub can grow to 6 feet tall and produces lightly scented yellow flowers and black berries.

GENEST, fleur de

BROOM FLOWER

For love I endure   1/58 • 2/25

GENEST, la graine de

BROOM BERRY

I love the redhead   3/49 • 4/71

GENETREULLE

DYER'S BROOM   (Genista tinctoria)

Remember the good deed (or **kindness**)   3/49 • 4/71

Found in fields and woods, dyer's broom grows to about 3 feet high and produces bright yellow pea-like flowers from which a yellow dye can be made.

GENEVRE

JUNIPER   (Juniperus)

Take good care   3/49 • 4/71

There are a number of species of juniper, from low spreading shrubs with long, trailing branches to trees over 120 feet tall. All are evergreen conifers with needle-like leaves.

GIROFLÉE BLANCHE
 WHITE STOCK, WHITE GILLYFLOWER   (Matthiola incana)
 Chaste love   1/58 • 2/25 • 3/49 • 4/71
 See also: VIOLIER BLANC
 Known as common stock, hoary stock, ten week stock or gillyflower,
Matthiola incana is native to the coast of southern Europe. Many
varieties of gillyflower are heavily scented.

GIROFFLÉE GRISE
 GREY STOCK, GREY GILLYFLOWER
 My heart is all yours   3/49 • 4/71

GIROFLÉE ROUGE
 RED STOCK, RED GILLYFLOWER
 Beauty   1/58 • 2/25
 Excellent beauty   3/49 • 4/71
 See also: VIOLIER ROUGE

GIROFFLÉE DE PRAIRIE ou DE MURAILLE
 WALLFLOWER   (Erysimum cheiri)
 I have good will and love for you   3/49 • 4/71
 Growing throughout Europe on old walls and among rocks,
wallflowers come in a variety of shades of yellow, red and brown.

GIRON
 *CUCKOO PINT, LORDS AND LADIES   (Arum maculatum)
 Var: Girond
 Falsehood   1/58 • 2/25
 Falsehood and deceit   3/49 • 4/71

A common hedgerow plant, cuckoo pint grows to about 2 feet 6 inches tall and puts out a purple spike from which a cluster of bright red berries develops. The root was used by the 1st century Greek physician Dioscorides to make an ointment to treat gout. In the Middle Ages, the plant was believed to be effective in treating plague and the leaves were used to treat boils and ulcers. It remained in use in various medications into the 17th century.

GLAYEUL
GLADIOLUS   (Gladiolus)
Honour   3/49 • 4/71
The wild gladiolus native to the Mediterranean region is less spectacular than the gladioli that were brought from South Africa in the 17th and 18th centuries and were cultivated to produce the garden flowers we know today.

GLAYEUL, la fleur de
GLADIOLUS FLOWER
Banquet   3/49 • 4/71

GRASE
NOT IDENTIFIED
Without hope   3/49 • 4/71

GRASSE GESINE
NOT IDENTIFIED
Don't expect me   3/49 • 4/71
Gesine is a term for a lying-in bed, or for being in labour, so it's possible that this plant was used medicinally to aid pregnant women.

But, unfortunately, I haven't been able to identify it.

GROSELIER

CURRANT   (Ribes)

Var: Groisillier blanc

You want to change   1/58 • 2/25 • 3/49 • 4/71

White currants were being cultivated in Russia in the 11th century but red currants were only domesticated in the 15th century and black currants not until the 17th. Wild currants, however, were used medicinally and for flavouring and colouring of food and wine.

GROISILLIER ROUGE

RED CURRANT

Lechery   3/49 • 4/71

GUARAS

SPINDLE TREE   (Euonymus europaeus)

Var: Garais, Garai

It annoys me too much   1/58

You annoy me too much   3/49 • 4/71

The spindle tree can grow to a height of 20 feet and live for over 100 years. Its bark, which is green, darkens as it gets older and, in winter, it produces bright pink fruit with orange seeds. Its wood has been used to make things as diverse as musical instruments, spindles and skewers.

GUY

MISTLETOE   (Viscum album)

Without any help   1/58 • 2/25 • 3/49 • 4/71

Mistletoe can grow on many trees including apple, hawthorn, oak, elm, pear, willow and walnut. It used to be the custom in France for young men to herald the start of a new year by carrying around branches of mistletoe.

GUI, graine de
   MISTLETOE BERRY
   Var: La graine de guy
   The fair one   1/58
   I love the fair one   3/49 • 4/71

HERBE COMMUNE

COMMON GRASS

Let's change our minds   1/58 • 2/25

Let's change the subject   3/49 • 4/71

HERBE FLEURIE

FLOWERING GRASS

That pleases me   3/49 • 4/71

HERBE NOÜÉE d'un noeud ou de plusieurs

KNOTGRASS   (Polygonum aviculare)

Can I not despair of your love   3/49 • 4/71

Knotgrass can grow to about 16 inches high and is found in fields and on waste ground. It has white flowers.

HERBE S. JEAN ou LIERRE TERRESTRE

GROUND IVY   (Glechoma hederacea)

I desire you   3/49 • 4/71

Ground ivy is a creeping perennial that, for many centuries, was valued as a medicinal herb but is now more likely to be regarded as a weed since it establishes itself in lawns and is hard to eradicate. When mown, it smells like mint. It likes moist, shady habitats, especially woodlands and waste ground, and produces funnel shaped flowers that range from blue to violet. For centuries it was recommended as a treatment for a variety of conditions including conjunctivitis, tinnitus, kidney problems, indigestion and bronchitis. It was also grown in kitchen gardens as a salad leaf and was used to preserve ale. The leaves are toxic to horses and some other animals.

HERBE SENSITIVE

MIMOSA, SENSITIVE PLANT   (Mimosa pudica)

You are admirable   3/49 • 4/71

There are a number of species of sensitive plant but none is native to Europe. Most come from South America but some are from the East Indies and the Levant. I have not been able to discover when mimosa arrived in Europe but the French scientist Jean-Jacques d'Ortous de Mairan (1678-1771) made a study of its properties, which suggests that it may have been quite newly introduced when listed in Les Oracles Divertissans. De Mairan's study concerned the plant's ability to fold its leaves in and droop when touched or when darkness falls.

HERMINETTES

*GARDEN PINK   (Dianthus plumarius)

I shall never forget you   1/58 • 3/49 • 4/71

See also: OEILLET, FEUILLE D'

'Erminette' is a vernacular name for the pink in some parts of France, although the common name by which this plant is known is mignardise. The flowers can be double or single, and a variety of shades between white and purple. They are always sweet scented.

HIEBLE

DANEWORT, DWARF ELDER   (Sambucus ebulus)

Convenience   3/49 • 4/71

Found in hedgerows and on waste ground, this plant can grow to around 6 feet tall and has flat-topped clusters of small white flowers.

HOUBLON

HOPS   (Humulus lupulus)

That which you wish   3/49 • 4/71

See also: SERPENTINE

Wild hops are found in hedges and thickets but can grow to a height of over 25 feet, especially when cultivated. The Romans grew hops for the young shoots, which they ate as a vegetable. The hop fruits have been used in brewing since about the 11th century. In the 16th century hops were regarded as an important medicinal herb and were used to treat conditions such as jaundice and venereal disease.

HOUX

HOLLY   (Ilex aquifolium)

Harshness (or **rudeness**)   1/58 • 2/25 • 3/49 • 4/71

Holly (of which there are numerous species) has the whitest of all the hard woods. It has been used for veneering furniture, sometimes stained to imitate ebony. As a heraldic emblem, it symbolises truth.

HOUX, graine de

HOLLY BERRY

I love the fair one   1/58 • 2/25

I love the redhead   3/49 • 4/71

HYACINTE

HYACINTH   (Hyacinthus orientalis)
or HYACINTH BLUEBELL   (Delphinium ajacis)
I am beautiful and good   3/49 • 4/71
This entry may refer either to the hyacinth (Hyacinthus orientalis) which is native to western Syria and Turkey and was brought to western Europe around the middle of the 16th century, or to the hyacinth bluebell (Delphinium ajacis) which is native to Europe.

JALOUSIE

*BLACK VANILLA ORCHID (Gymnadenia nigra)

Extreme pain 1/58 • 2/25 • 3/49 • 4/71

This vernacular name has been given to a number of plants but, here, is most likely to refer to the black vanilla orchid which is native to the mountainous regions of Europe.

JAUNEROTES

CHANTERELLE, GIROLLE (Cantharellus cibarius)

Var: Jannerotes, Jagnotte

Villainy 1/58 • 2/25 • 3/49 • 4/71

The chanterelle mushroom grows in temperate forests. It was first discovered as being good to eat in the 16th century, probably in France and, by the 18th century, it had become an established part of French cuisine.

JOBARDE

HOUSELEEK (Sempervivum tectorum)

Jealousy 3/49 • 4/71

This succulent whose leaves form clusters of rosettes, grows on rocks and on the roofs of houses. Also known as hen-and-chickens, it produces clusters of star-shaped reddish-purple flowers. The ancient

Romans believed that a building which had houseleeks growing on it would be protected from lightning strikes.

JONC, un brin de

    RUSH, ONE STEM   (Juncus)

    Righteousness   1/58 • 2/25

    Innocence and righteousness   3/49 • 4/71

    Innocence and doctrine   X1/64

    There are many species of rush, all in the Juncus genus. Juncus effusus (the common rush) is a perennial, flowering rush which grows profusely in wet surroundings.

JONC, deux brins de

    RUSH, TWO STEMS

    Mutual love   1/58 • 3/49 • 4/71

KAROTTES

CARROTS   (Daucus carota subsp. sativus)
Enough for you (or, possibly, **You are enough**)   1/58 • 2/25
See also: PASTONNADES ou CAROTTES

LAICT AU COCU

SPURGE   (Euphorbia)

Deception   3/49 • 4/71

There are numerous species of spurge, including annual and perennial plants as well as shrubs and trees. Most have a very poisonous milky sap. Two species that are native to Europe are the wood spurge (E. amygdaloides), a bushy evergreen perennial, and the cypress spurge (E. cyparissias), a low growing plant used for ground cover. Both of these produce yellow flowers.

LANDE

COMMON GORSE   (Ulex europaeus)

Useless curiosity   3/49 • 4/71

Growing on heathland and waste ground, gorse is a bushy, spiny shrub that grows to a height of around 6 feet and whose yellow flowers smell like coconut.

LANDE FLEURIE

FLOWERING GORSE

Repentance   3/49 • 4/71

LANGUE DE CHIEN

GYPSYFLOWER   (Cynoglossum officinale)

Envy   3/49 • 4/71

Also known as hound's tongue, gypsyflower grows on waste land and on the edges of roads and fields. It has reddish-purple, funnel-shaped flowers. An English vernacular name for it is 'rats and mice' because of its smell.

LANGUE DE PIVERT, fleur de

HAIRY WOODRUSH   (Luzula pilosa)

Var: Fleur de langue de pivett

You will get what you ask for   1/58 • 3/49 • 4/71

This is a short, grass-like flowering perennial, which is a member of the rush family.

LAUREOLLE

SPURGE LAUREL   (Daphne laureola)

or ROSE DAPHNE   (Daphne cneorum)

It will never happen to me   3/49 • 4/71

See also: AUREOLLE

Spurge-laurel (D. laureola), which is neither a spurge nor a laurel, despite its name, is a bushy evergreen shrub with dark green shiny leaves and greenish yellow flowers. Rose daphne (D. cneorum) is a low-growing trailing evergreen shrub which produces dense clusters of sweet smelling pink flowers.

LAURIER

LAUREL, BAY   (Laurus nobilis)
Victory   1/58 • 2/25
Certain happiness   3/49 • 4/71
An evergreen shrub or tree, the laurel was a symbol of victory and accomplishment in Roman times. Laurel wreaths were awarded to the winners of games and contests. A widely-held belief that laurel could not be struck by lightning led to the Emperor Tiberius always wearing a wreath of laurel whenever there was a storm.

LAURIER COUPPÉE, fueille de
LEAF OF CUT LAUREL
I lack the power   1/58 • 2/25 • 3/49 • 4/71

LAURIER, les feüilles et rinceaux de
LEAVES AND BRANCHES OF LAUREL
Complete victory   3/49 • 4/71

LAURIER, GRAINE DE
BERRY OF LAUREL
I love the redhead   1/58 • 2/25
I love the brunette   3/49 • 4/71

LAVANDE
LAVENDER   (Lavandula angustifolia)
Work   1/58 • 2/25 • 3/49 • 4/71
See also: ASPIC, FEUILLE D'

LAVANDE COTONNÉE

LAVENDER COTTON   (Santolina chamaecyparissus)

Var: Lavande coutonnée

You talk too much   1/58 • 2/25 • 3/49 • 4/71

Known in English either as lavender cotton or cotton lavender, this low growing shrub has narrow silver leaves and long-stemmed bright yellow button-like flowers.

LECTUE

LETTUCE   (Lactuca sativa)

Var: Laictues, Lactues

Good news   1/58 • 2/25 • 3/49 • 4/71

Lettuce is known to have been cultivated by the ancient Egyptians and, later, by the Greeks and Romans. By the first century CE many varieties were known. Several mediaeval herbals mention lettuce.

LETTRONS

MILK THISTLE, SOW THISTLE   (Sonchus oleraceus)

Var: Laicterons

You are too stupid and too young   1/58

Stupid and young   3/49 • 4/71

This plant has long narrow, lobed leaves with spines along their edges. It produces clusters of yellow, dandelion-like flowers which develop into fluffy white seedheads.

LIN

FLAX, LINSEED   (Linum usitatissimum)

Var: L'if [Yew tree]. This variation is found in 3/49 and 4/71. It seems likely that this was a misprint which was then copied in the later volume, rather than the deliberate transfer of the meaning ('good household') to a different plant.

Good household   1/58 • 2/25 • 3/49 • 4/71

Flax has been cultivated since ancient times, linen being woven from its fibre and oil being extracted from its crushed seeds. The plants grow to about 4 feet tall and produce pale blue five-petalled flowers.

LUNAIRE

HONESTY   (Lunaria annua or Lunaria rediviva)

Your heart is too secret   3/49 • 4/71

A hardy annual or biennial, its name derives from the Latin word for 'moon' (luna) and relates to the flat, round, silvery seed pods that develop from its clusters of purple flowers.

LYERRE

IVY   (Hedera helix)

Var: Lierre

Ingratitude   1/58 • 2/25 • 3/49 • 4/71

Venerated by the ancients, ivy was believed to prevent intoxication – which is why the Roman god Bacchus is depicted wearing it as a crown.

LYS

LILY   (Lilium - numerous species)

Faith   1/58 • 2/25

LYS, la feüille de

LILY LEAF

I don't know it   3/49 • 4/71

LYS BLANCHE, la fleur de

MADONNA LILY   (Lilium candidum)

Joy and beauty   3/49 • 4/71

Probably a native of the Balkans and the Middle East, the Madonna lily has been cultivated for over 3000 years and was the first lily to find its way into European gardens. It is depicted in a fresco excavated from the ruins of the palace at Knossos (now in the Heraklion Archaeological Museum) dating from around 1500 BCE. The Romans distributed the Madonna lily throughout their empire, the Greeks made an ointment from it and both used the bulb as a vegetable. Symbolising chastity, it was associated with the Virgin Mary from the early days of Christianity and appears in many mediaeval artworks and stained glass windows.

LYS DE VALLÉE

LILY OF THE VALLEY   (Convallaria majalis)

Purity   3/49 • 4/71

See also: MUGUET

Lily of the valley has been grown in gardens for at least 3000 years. The flowers were often used in mediaeval times to decorate Lady chapels and statues of the Virgin Mary. Extracts have been used to treat headaches, hysteria and fainting.

LYS JAUNE

YELLOW DAY LILY   (Hemerocallis lilioasphodelus)

Honour and pre-eminence   3/49 • 4/71

Although it probably originated in Asia, the day lily has long been found in Europe and was a common garden flower in the 17th century. It has lemon yellow trumpet-shaped flowers which exude a strong perfume.

LYVESCHE

LOVAGE   (Levisticum officinale)

Var: Liveche

Come forward   1/58 • 3/49 • 4/71

A tall, perennial plant with flat-topped clusters of greenish-yellow flowers, lovage is probably native to the south of France and has long been cultivated in Europe as a herb (the leaves), a vegetable (the roots) and a spice (the seeds).

MACRE, la fleur de

WATER CHESTNUT FLOWER   (Trapa natans)

Covert betrayal   3/49 • 4/71

The water chestnut has been cultivated in China and India for its edible fruit for at least 3000 years and, by Roman times, was being used in parts of Europe to make bread. As its name indicates, it is an aquatic plant and it grows in stagnant or slow-moving fresh water.

MACRE, le fruit de

FRUIT OF THE WATER CHESTNUT

Danger from all sides   3/49 • 4/71

MANDRAGORE

MANDRAKE   (Mandragora officinarum)

Literally **Generative coupling** [Generative conjonction] but presumably meaning **Sexual intercourse**   3/49 • 4/71

Legends have always surrounded the mandrake whose roots are said to resemble a human form. Mediaeval herbals show a male version with a long beard and a female with long hair. Although toxic, it was for centuries used as a pain-killer and a sleeping aid.

MANTE

MINT   (Mentha)

Var: Mente

Reverie   1/58 • 2/25

See also: MENTASTRE, MENTE NOIRE, MENTE AQUATIQUE, MENTE BLANCHE

The species of mint native to Europe include wild mint (M. sylvestris), meadow mint (M. pratensis), sweet mint (M. suavis), spearmint (M. viridis) and peppermint (M. piperita).

MARGRITES

DAISIES   (Bellis perennis)

Var: Marguerites, Marguerite

A good time   1/58 • 2/25

Give yourself a good time   3/49 • 4/71

The common daisy used to be incorporated into ointments for treating aches and pains, cleaning wounds and stopping bleeding. By the late 16th century, double varieties and red varieties were known.

MARGRITE SEULE

SINGLE DAISY

Always good hope   1/58

MARGUERITE GRISE

GREY DAISY

Be satisfied   3/49 • 4/71

MARGUERITE ROUGE

RED DAISY

Good hope   3/49 • 4/71

MARGRITE CHAMPESTRE

FIELD DAISY

Var: Marguerite champestre

I am unable to provide   [je ne suis à pourvoir]   1/58

I'm privileged   [je suis pourveüe]   3/49 • 4/71

'Pourvoir' and 'pourveüe' are perhaps similar enough to suggest that
the change of meaning may have been a misprint.

MARGRITE BLANCHE

OX EYE DAISY   (Leucanthemum vulgare)

Var: Marguerites blanche, Marguerite blanche

I shall think (or dream) about it   1/58 • 2/25 • 3/49 • 4/71

Growing up to 27 inches in height and found on grassland and
in pastures throughout Europe, the ox eye daisy was widely used in
mediaeval medicine.

MARJOLAINE MENUE

SMALL MARJORAM   (Origanum)

Goodness   1/58 • 2/25 • 3/49 • 4/71

It is not entirely clear what is meant by 'menue' and 'grosse' in this
entry and the one that follows. However, it is possible that one is sweet
marjoram (O. majorana) and the other wild marjoram (O. vulgare). The
ancient Greeks and Romans used wild marjoram as a herb. By the
Middle Ages it was being used medicinally to treat a variety of ailments
including toothache, indigestion and joint pain.

MARJOLAINE GROSSE
LARGE MARJORAM
Lying   1/58 • 2/25 • 3/49 • 4/71

MAROÜET
BASTARD CHAMOMILE   (Helichrysum stoechas)
You offend yourself   3/49 • 4/71
An annual or perennial shrub that lives on dry, rocky or sandy soil, bastard (or false) chamomile can grow to about 4 feet in height and spread to over 3 feet. Its flowers, which it produces in round clusters, are very small and bright yellow.

MARTAGON
TURK'S CAP LILY   (Lilium martagon)
You are beautiful and humble   3/49 • 4/71
This handsome lily which produces spikes of pink to purple flowers was very popular in 16th century gardens. It grows wild in woods and pastures and on the mountains of central and southern Europe.

MASTIC
MASTIC TREE (or ITS RESIN)   (Pistacia lentiscus)
Love me   1/58 • 2/25 • 3/49 • 4/71
An evergreen shrub or small tree, mastic produces an aromatic resin which has long been used to whiten teeth and sweeten the breath. The wood is aromatic when burned, and the berries produce oil which can be used in lamps.

MAULVES, fleur de

MALLOW   (Malva)

Var: Fleur ou feüille de mauves [flower or leaf of mallows]

You will get out of misery   1/58 • 3/49 • 4/71

There are many species of mallow that are native to Europe, including the musk scented mallow (M. moschata) and the common mallow (M. rotundifolia) which thrives on waste ground and beside roads. The common mallow grows to a height of about 4 feet, has pink or mauve flowers, and was used as a vegetable by the Romans.

MELINEUF

** HONEYWORT

I will not give you leave   3/49 • 4/71

The closest I could come to 'melineuf' was melinet, a name for honeywort (Cerinthe major). The cultivated version has bluish leaves and clusters of deep blue tubular bell-like flowers and it has been grown in gardens since the Middle Ages. The flowers of the wild version can be any colour between white and purple.

MELLIER

MEDLAR   (Mespilus germanica)

Sounds of mercy [sons misericorde]   3/49

Without mercy [sans misericorde]   X1/64 • 4/71

Since 'without mercy' makes more sense than 'sounds of mercy' it is likely that the earlier version was a misprint, which was corrected in the later volumes. A large shrub or small tree, the medlar has been cultivated for its fruit since Roman times. However, the fruit can only be eaten raw once it has been bletted – that is, allowed to become over-ripe.

MENTASTRE ou MENTE SAUVAGE
MINT OR WILD MINT

Var: Mantastre ou mente sauvage

I wish you well 3/49 • 4/71

See also: MANTE

Two forms of European wild mint are Mentha sylvestris and Mentha arvensis, both of which like moist soils.

MENTE AQUATIQUE
WATER MINT (Mentha aquatica)

Leave everything 3/49 • 4/71

See also: MANTE

This plant is commonly found in water-logged ground.

MENTE BLANCHE
APPLE MINT Mentha suaveolens)

or HOREHOUND (Marrubium vulgare)

Write to me 3/49 • 4/71

See also: MANTE

Apple mint (Mentha suaveolens) is also known as pineapple mint. Horehound (Marrubium vulgare) is a member of the mint family and is known to have been used medicinally, particularly for respiratory problems, as far back as the 1st century BCE.

MENTE NOIRE
Literally: BLACK MINT

A happy alliance 3/49 • 4/71

See also: MANTE

I have been unable to determine which species of mint this relates to.

MEURIER

MULBERRY   (Morus)

Perfect love   1/58 • 2/25

Certain lineage and perfect love   3/49 • 4/71

Both 3/49 and 4/71 include the following paragraph, offering an additional meaning:

"Le Meurier also means wisdom, prudence, certain profit, for among all the trees it is the last one to sprout its leaves, and the only one that never fails to bear fruit. It is the opposite of the almond tree whose flowers, blooming early, are often burned by frosts or snows, and which only bears fruit by chance, compelling the Sages to give it the name of harebrained and fool."

The Chinese were the first to cultivate mulberry trees in order to provide food for silkworms. Both black mulberries (M. nigra) and white mulberries (M. alba) were grown by the Romans who used the leaves to treat conditions of the mouth, throat and lungs. In the 17th century the bark was used as a purgative to expel tapeworms from the intestines.

MEURIER, feüille de

MULBERRY LEAF

Covert betrayal   3/49 • 4/71

MILLE FUEILLE

YARROW   (Achillea millefolium)

It (or **he**) **bores me**   1/58 • 2/25 • 3/49 • 4/71

See also: ACILLETS & REJOINTE

MILLE-PERTUIS

ST JOHN'S WORT (Hypericum perforatum)

You don't keep anything secret 3/49 • 4/71

Growing wild in groves, hedges and thickets, St John's wort has yellow star-shaped flowers with numerous stamens. It has been used medicinally since ancient times to treat a wide variety of complaints, particularly wounds, skin problems and depression. Hypericum ointment is still widely available (often mixed with Calendula – marigold – which can also help to heal damaged skin). Scientific trials in recent years have shown that not only is Hypericum as effective in treating depression as synthetic anti-depressants, but it has fewer side effects.

MILLET

MILLET (Panicum miliaceum)

or CRABGRASS (Digitaria sanguinalis)

Do not approach that 3/49 • 4/71

I found three translations of 'millet' – maize (Zea mays), millet (Panicum miliaceum), and common crabgrass (Digitaria sanguinalis). The first of these is native to Mexico and was probably first cultivated in Europe in the early to mid 16th century in Spain, so I think this is less likely to be the plant indicated here. Millet was growing wild in Greece as early as 3000 BCE and its cultivation in Europe began around 1500 BCE. Crabgrass is native to Europe and, although now considered to be a weed, used to be grown for animal feed.

MOLAINE

MULLEIN

Var: Molaine ou topasse

Delicacy   1/58 • 2/25

You are delicate (or **dainty**)   3/49 • 4/71

See also: BOUILLON BLANC & VERMINEUSE

Topasse translates as 'topaz'. I have been unable to determine whether this is another name for mullein or whether it is the name of a different plant.

MORELLE

NIGHTSHADE   (Solanum)

I only think good of it   3/49 • 4/71

There are many species of nightshade. In Europe woody nightshade or bittersweet (S. dulcamara) is well known. It can grow to over 6 feet high and produces purple flowers and bright red berries.

MORRON

SCARLET PIMPERNEL   (Anagallis arvensis)

or CHICKWEED   (Stellaria media)

Var: Moron

You are too boring [vous estes trop ennuyeux]   1/58 • 4/71

You are too envious [vous estes trop envieux]   2/25 • 3/49

This is another example of a change in a couple of letters – possibly a misprint – changing the meaning. Scarlet pimpernel (Anagallis arvensis) is known as mouron (or moron) rouge, while chickweed (Stellaria media) is mouron (or moron) des oiseaux. Both are common wildflowers.

MORSURE DU DIABLE ou FAULSE SCABIEUSE

DEVIL'S BIT (or FALSE) SCABIOUS   (Succisa pratensis)

You brought it to me   3/49 • 4/71

See also: SCABIEUSE

Growing in bogs and wet places, this plant has a stump-like root from which it gets its name. The legend goes that this was a valuable herb for mankind but that the Devil, resenting this, took a bite out of the root to put an end to its usefulness. The dried leaves of the plant have been used to dye wool a yellowish-green.

MOUSSE BLANCHE

WHITE MOSS   (Leucobryum)

Var: Mousse blanche ou grise

Old age   1/58 • 2/25 • 3/49 • 4/71

See also: MOUSSE VERDE

Some 12,000 species of moss are known. Moss has been used over the centuries as insulation both for buildings and in clothes. White moss usually refers to the genus Leucobryum, otherwise known as pincushion moss, which forms what looks like large grey-white puncushions in wet woodlands or swamps.

MOUSSE VERDE

GREEN MOSS

Var: Mousse herbue ou verde

Laziness   1/58 • 3/49 • 4/71

MUGUET

LILY OF THE VALLEY   (Convallaria majalis)

Var: Muguet blanc

Better and better   1/58 • 2/25 • 3/49 • 4/71

See also: LYS DE VALLÉE

MUGUET BLEU

**LILAC CHASTE TREE   (Vitex agnus-castus)

Youth in love   3/49 • 4/71

There are several candidates for this but the most likely seems to be
Vitex agnus-castus, the lilac chaste tree. A native of the Mediterranean
region, this small tree was considered by the Romans to be sacred to the
virgin goddess Vesta. Its spikes of lavender coloured flowers are sweet
smelling and attract butterflies.

MYRRE

GARDEN MYRRH   (Myrrhis odorata)

Var: Myrrhe

Recovery   1/58 • 2/25 • 3/49 • 4/71

Once widely used medicinally, this is an aniseed scented perennial that
produces flat-topped clusters of white flowers.

NARCISSE ou FLEUR DE JANVIER

NARCISSUS, DAFFODIL   (Narcissus)

Gay joy in humility   1/58 • 2/25 • 3/49 • 4/71

There are numerous species of narcissus, many of which were known by the late 16th century, when they became very popular. A lot of these old species are still available today.

NAVEAU

TURNIP   (Brassica rapa)

Expense   3/49 • 4/71

Eaten as a vegetable by the ancient Greeks and Romans, over the centuries the turnip has served as a food for both humans and animals.

NERPRUN

WATER LILY   (Nymphaea or Nuphar)

Soon   3/49 • 4/71

Two genus of plants, Nymphaea and Nuphar, are classed as water lilies. The common white water lily (Nymphaea alba) is the only one of its genus native to Europe. The common yellow water lily (Nuphar lutea) is also native to Europe and can be found in ditches, lakes and slow running rivers.

NERPRUN, graine de
WATER LILY BERRY
I love the brunette   1/58 • 2/25 • 3/49 • 4/71

NIELLE
CORN COCKLE   (Agrostemma githago)
To love without being loved   3/49 • 4/71 • OD77
This weed, which tends to grow in cornfields, has narrow grey-green leaves and funnel shaped purple flowers.

NOISILLIER, les noisettes du
HAZEL NUTS
Rather to die   3/49 • 4/71
See also: COULDRE

NOIX
NUT
A game and play   3/49 • 4/71
See also: AMANDIER [almond], CHASTAIGNE [chestnuts], COULDRE & NOISILLIER [hazel nuts], FOUSTEAU [beech nuts], NOYER [walnut]
The word 'noix' used without a qualifying adjective can refer to nuts in general or, more specifically, to a walnut.

NOYER
WALNUT   (Juglans regia)
Persecuted innocence [innocence]   3/49 • 4/71
Persecuted innocent [innocente – probably a misprint] X1/64
People have been eating walnuts for more than 9000 years. In ancient

Rome they were dedicated to Jupiter while, in ancient Persia, only those of royal status were allowed to eat them. Walnut wood, which is hard, dark and finely grained, has long been popular with cabinet-makers.

NOYER, fueille de
   WALNUT LEAF
   Unburden me   1/58 • 2/25 • 3/49 • 4/71

OEILLET, feüille d'
PINK, LEAF OF   (Dianthus)
A game without villainy   3/49 • 4/71
See also: HERMINETTE

OIGNON
ONION   (Allium cepa)
Everything backwards   3/49 • 4/71
As an explanation of the meaning, both 3/49 and 4/71 include the following: "It is because the onion is smaller, and less strong when the moon is full, contrary to all other plants."
Onions were an important part of the diet of many early civilisations. The ancient Egyptians believed their rings of leaves represented eternal life and often placed them in tombs. In ancient Greece, athletes ate onions to improve their performance, while Roman gladiators rubbed onion juice onto their skin to tone their muscles.

OIGNON, fueille d'
ONION LEAF
Var: Oignon, feuille d'
I withdraw completely   1/58 • 3/49 • 4/71

OIGNON DE LYS, feuille d'

NOT IDENTIFIED

Through you I will know it   3/49 • 4/71

This may refer to a lily bulb.

OLIVIER, branche ou rameau d'

BRANCH OR BOUGH OF OLIVE TREE   (Olea europaea)

Let us make peace   3/49 • 4/71

Originally from Asia Minor, the olive has been cultivated for at least 5000 years. Its wood is very hard and its attractive colour and grain has made it popular with woodworkers and cabinet makers.

OLIVIER, fueille d'

OLIVE LEAF

No one but you will ever have me   1/58 • 2/25 • 3/49 • 4/71

ORANGER

ORANGE TREE   (Citrus aurantium)

You cost me too much   3/49 • 4/71

Native to Asia, orange trees were introduced to Spain by the Moors in the 10th century. In the 16th century, they were brought to the Mediterranean region by Italian and Portuguese merchants. The sweet orange rapidly became popular across Europe, and wealthy landowners built themselves orangeries in which to grow them.

ORANGE

ORANGE

Whatever it is worth, or whatever it costs   3/49 • 4/71

ORMEAU

 ELM TREE   (Ulmus minor)

Force   3/49 • 4/71

The common elm can grow to over 100 feet high. The bark has been used to treat skin complaints.

ORTIE

STINGING NETTLE   (Urtica dioica)

Treason   1/58 • 2/25 • 3/49 • 4/71

Nettles have been used medicinally since the Bronze Age. Roman soldiers are said to have used the nettle's sting to help them stay awake when on night duty. A fibre derived from nettles has been used (like the linen thread from flax) to make fabric which can be dyed or bleached like cotton.

OSEILLE ou VINETTE MENUE

*FIELD SORREL, SHEEP SORREL   (Rumex acetosella)

Think of my burning desire [songez à mon ardent desir]   3/49 • 4/71

Think of no burning desire [songez à non ardent desir – almost certainly a misprint]   X1/64

Literally "small sorrel", this probably refers to field sorrel or sheep sorrel. Sorrels are perennial herbaceous plants, commonly found in grassy habitats. All green leaved varieties are edible and several are cultivated.

OSEILLE GROSSE

*GARDEN SORREL   (Rumex acetosa)

Restoration   3/49 • 4/71

Literally "large sorrel", this probably refers to garden sorrel, a popular edible variety.

OSIER

WILLOW   (Salix)

Hope   3/49 • 4/71

See also: SAULE, SAULDRE BLANCHE & SAULDRE COMMUNE

There are about 400 species of willow trees and shrubs, mostly growing in cold and temperate regions. A number of species are native to Europe, such as the pussy willow (S. caprea) and the basket willow or common osier (S. viminalis). The weeping willow (S. babylonica) comes originally from China but was brought to Europe along the Silk Road. In ancient China, willow branches were believed to protect against evil.

PALME CHRISTI

*CASTOR OIL PLANT   (Ricinus communis)

A beautiful likeness   3/49 • 4/71

Native to the Mediterranean region, this is a fast growing shrub that can grow to about 40 feet tall. Its seeds are made into castor oil.

PALME NOSTRE DAME ou HERBE À LA POITRINE

NOT IDENTIFIED

Contrariness   3/49 • 4/71

PANAIS

PARSNIP   (Pastinaca sativa)

Poison   3/49 • 4/71

See also: PASTONNADES

Probably native to the Mediterranean region, the parsnip was used by the Romans both as a vegetable and in medications. It was also used as a sweetener before sugar from sugar beet and sugar cane became available.

PASSE ROSE

HOLLYHOCK   (Alcea rosea)

Var: Passe rose rouge [red hollyhock], Passerose

Please me   1/58 • 2/25 • 3/49 • 4/71

Hollyhocks have been grown in the gardens of both Europe and Asia for many centuries.

PASSE-ROSE BLANCHE
WHITE HOLLYHOCK
Gentleness and humility   3/49 • 4/71

PASSE VELOUX
GREEN AMARANTH   (Amaranthus viridis)
Var: Passe velours
Beauty without goodness   1/58 • 2/25 • 3/49 • 4/71
See also: AMARANTE & QUEUE DE RENARD
Possibly native to Asia, the green amaranth is an annual with spikes of tiny green flowers.

PASTONNADES ou CAROTTES
PARSNIPS or CARROTS   (Pastinaca sativa & Daucus carota)
False esteem   3/49 • 4/71
SEE ALSO PANAIS (PARSNIP) & KAROTTES

PATTE DE LOUP
BUGLEWEED, GIPSYWORT   (Lycopus europaeus)
Cruelty, pride and haughtiness   3/49 • 4/71
Also known as water horehound, bugleweed is a member of the mint family and is found throughout Europe in damp places beside ditches and rivers. It can be used to make a black permanent dye for linen, wool and silk. An old belief was that gypsies used it to stain their skin.

PATTE D'OURS

STINKING HELLEBORE   (Helleborus foetidus)

or HOGWEED   (Heracleum sphondylium)

You resemble him   3/49 • 4/71

See also: HELLEBORE

Patte d'ours (meaning 'bear's paw') is a name that has been given both to stinking hellebore and hogweed. The former grows to about 18 inches and has groups of drooping greenish flowers, while the latter can grow to over 6 feet and has flat topped clusters of white flowers.

PAVOT ROUGE, la fleur de

FLOWER OF RED POPPY   (Papaver rhoeas)

I don't know how to love in a better place   3/49 • 4/71

There are numerous species of poppies but the best known is probably the red corn poppy (Papaver rhoeas) which is native to Europe.

PAVOT BLANC, la fleur de

FLOWER OF WHITE POPPY   (Papaver somniferum)

I only think of you   3/49 • 4/71

This probably relates to the opium poppy which was being grown in the Mediterranean region and in southwest Asia by the 5th millennium BCE. The Sumerians called it the 'joy plant'.

PENSÉES

PANSIES   (Viola tricolor)

Sometimes boredom   1/58 • 2/25 • 3/49 • 4/71

Also known in English as heartsease, the pansy has been grown in gardens since the Middle Ages and appears in many mediaeval illuminations.

PENSEE SEULE
SINGLE PANSY
You wait for me   1/58

PENSÉES, bouquet de plusieurs
BUNCH OF PANSIES
I wait for you, or It's in you   3/49 • 4/71

PENTECOUSTE BLANCHE, la fleur de
*WHITE HONEYSUCKLE FLOWER
I wish to serve you   3/49 • 4/71
See also: CHEVRE FEUILLE
The name 'pentecote' has been given to several plants including some types of orchid, the cuckoo flower (Cardamine pratensis) and honeysuckle. In view of the fact that, here, 'pentecouste' is described as white, red or violet, the more versatile honeysuckle seems the most likely.

PENTECOUSTE ROUGE, la fleur de
*RED HONEYSUCKLE FLOWER
Your presence gives me pain   3/49 • 4/71

PENTECOUSTE VIOLETTE, la fleur de
*PURPLE HONEYSUCKLE FLOWER
I take pleasure in your presence   3/49 • 4/71

PERCEPIERRE
*SAMPHIRE   (Crithmum maritimum)
Pain   3/49 • 4/71
Although some sources give the name 'percepierre' to other plants,

the most common attribution I found was to samphire. Also known as sea fennel, it grows on the rocky shores of the Mediterranean coastline. Shakespeare mentioned it in 'King Lear' with a reference to the danger of gathering it from cliffs.

PERELLE
DOCK   (Rumex)
Var: Parelle
Short expedition   1/58 • 3/49 • 4/71
Several species of dock are native to Europe. Often found growing near nettles, it is well known that the application of a dock leaf to a nettle sting can relieve the discomfort.

PERSIL
PARSLEY   (Petroselinum crispum)
My pain pleases me   1/58 • 3/49 • 4/71
My pain pleases   2/25
Probably native to the eastern Mediterranean region, parsley was believed by the ancient Greeks to have sprung from the blood of the fallen hero Archemorus, and was used to decorate tombs. It was used for culinary purposes throughout Europe in the Middle Ages. But even before it was cultivated for food, parsley was used as a medication for a variety of conditions including digestive problems, bronchitis and toothache.

PESCHE
PEACH   (Prunus persica)
You have a cold heart   3/49 • 4/71
The peach tree probably originated in China where it was

domesticated as early as 6000 BCE. By the 3rd century BCE it had arrived in Greece from where it spread to the rest of Europe.

PESCHER, fleur de
PEACH BLOSSOM
To pray for what you desire   1/58 • 2/25
I beseech you, or Youth, beauty & love   3/49 • 4/71

PICCOURT ou RANICULE
*STRAW OR STEM
Var: Picourt ou ranicule
Better times (or **Other times were better**)   3/49 • 4/71 • 4/71

PICQUE MADAME
NOT IDENTIFIED
Var: Piguemadame
I want to sleep with you   1/58 • 3/49 • 4/71

PIED D'ALOUETTE
LARKSPUR, DELPHINIUM   (Delphinium)
Beautiful and slim   3/49 • 4/71
Both the English 'larkspur' and the French name (literally 'lark's foot') relate to the long spur on the flower which looks like the talon of a lark. There are a number of species, one of which, D. staphisagria, was used by the ancient Greeks and Romans to make ointments. Since the mid 16th century larkspur has been grown in gardens for its decorative bright blue flowers.

PIMANT

LEMON BALM, COMMON BALM

Var: Pigment ou melisse

Pain   1/58 • 3/49 • 4/71

See also: BAUSME

PIMPENELLE

BURNET   (Sanguisorba minor)

Var: Pimpinnelle, Pimpernelle

You will have food   1/58

You have food   2/25

Food (or **nourishment**)   3/49 • 4/71

A perennial herb with a delicate cucumber flavour, burnet is also known as salad burnet or garden burnet. Growing in chalky and alkaline soils, it has rosettes of evergreen leaves, and its crimson flowers are attractive to numerous insects. As well as being used as a salad leaf and a flavouring for vinegar and drinks, it has in the past been used medicinally to staunch bleeding and to relieve diarrhoea.

PIN

PINE TREE   (Pinus)

You will die   3/49 • 4/71

There are many species of pine. Most are trees, although a few are shrubs. They are evergreen, coniferous and resin-producing, and most grow to 150 feet high or more. Since pines can live for many centuries, some surviving for over 1000 years, the meaning given to it here seems rather inappropriate.

PIN, feüilles de
PINE NEEDLES
Diverse thoughts   3/49 • 4/71

PINEAUX
*PINEAPPLE   (Ananas comosus)
Var: Pineaux ou pignons
Softness (or sweetness)   1/58 • 2/25 • 3/49 • 4/71
Although I found variations of 'pineaux' (pineau and pineux), I couldn't find the word as spelled here. Pineau was the name of a type of grape and can also mean grape seeds, while pineux means pine nuts. However, pignon (given as an alternative name by 3/49) translates as 'the kernell of a pine-apple'. The pineapple is believed to have originated in the Brazilian rainforests. Columbus brought it back to Spain, giving it the name 'piña' because it looks like a pine cone. Pineapples reached the rest of Europe in the 16th century and became very popular. A late 17th century painting in the Royal Collection shows King Charles II being presented with the first pineapple to be grown in England.

PLANTAIN
PLANTAIN   (Plantago major)
Var: Plantin
I am all yours   1/58 • 2/25 • 3/49 • 4/71
Plantains are annual and perennial herbs that tend to grow in grassy places, with low rosettes of leaves and long spikes of tiny greenish-yellow flowers. Some species have a long history of being used medicinally for various problems including the treatment of wounds.

POIRIER

PEAR TREE   (Pyrus communis)

In you lies too great an imperfection   1/58

Too great an imperfection   3/49 • 4/71

The pear is native to Europe and grows wild in woods and hedges, particularly in France and Germany.

POIRES SAUVAGES

WILD PEARS

You surprised me   3/49 • 4/71

POIS, feüilles de

PEA LEAF   (Lathyrus)

Bounty and good cheer   3/49 • 4/71

The pea was one of the first plants to be cultivated and evidence of its use as food goes back for millennia. There are numerous species.

POIX, fleur de

PEA FLOWER

I hold you back   1/58 • 2/25

I keep you to myself   3/49 • 4/71

POIX, gousse de

PEA POD

Var: Cosse de pois

I hold you in love and faith   1/58 • 3/49 • 4/71

POLLIOT

PENNYROYAL   (Mentha pulegium)

Var: Pouliot ou serpolet

Hinder and delay   1/58 • 2/25

Hindrance and delay   3/49 • 4/71

Pennyroyal, which has small leaves and whorls of lilac coloured flowers, grows in wet places such as ditches and bogs. It has a strong scent and, in ancient times, was used as a strewing herb to ward off fleas. A wreath of it worn on the head was believed to relieve dizziness while sprigs hung in a bedroom were thought to promote the good health of the occupant. In a 12th century herbal, it was also recommended as a cure for gout.

POLLIPODE

COMMON POLYPODY   (Polypodium vulgare)

Agreement   3/49 • 4/71

Polypody is an evergreen fern that grows to a height of about 12 inches.

POMMIER

APPLE TREE   (Malus domestica)

Var: Pomier, Feuille et fleur de pommier

I endure too much   1/58 • 2/25 • 3/49 • 4/71

The apple was cultivated by the Romans, and 22 varieties were known by the 1st century CE.

POMME

APPLE

Danger of dying from it   3/49 • 4/71

PORÉE OU POREAUX

*LEEK   (Allium porrum)

Var: Porés ou poreaux

For one pleasure, a thousand pains   3/49 • 4/71

Leeks were being eaten in Egypt as early as the second millennium BCE and are mentioned in the Bible (Numbers 11:5) as something the Israelites remembered eating there during their years of captivity. What has been dubbed 'the world's first cookbook', a collection of Roman recipes entitled 'De re culinaria' contains four recipes for leeks as well as a suggestion that leeks should be served as a vegetable in their own right (unlike onions which were only used for seasoning).

POTIRON

PUMPKIN   (Cucurbita maxima)

An abundance of good things   3/49 • 4/71

See also: CYTREULLE

POURPIE

PURSLANE   (Portulaca oleracea)

Var: Pourpié, Pourpier

Cold love   1/58 • 2/25 • 3/49 • 4/71

Purslane is a succulent which produces single yellow flowers that open for just a few hours on sunny mornings.

PRIMEVERE

COWSLIP   (Primula vulgaris)

or OXLIP   (Primula veris)

or PRIMROSE   (Primula elatior)

Var: Primeverre

I expect too much   1/58

I have waited too long or Young beauty   3/49 • 4/71

Cowslip, oxlip and primrose are all species of Primula. The primrose has long-stemmed yellow flowers and has been grown in gardens since the 15th century or earlier. The cowslip has clusters of scented flowers. The oxlip is similar to the cowslip but unscented.

PRUNIER

PLUM TREE   (Prunus domestica)

Desire to achieve   1/58 • 2/25 • 3/49 • 4/71

The plum tree may have originated in Asia Minor. Pliny, writing in the 1st century CE, says that it came to Italy via Syria and Greece. The wood has been used over the years to make furniture and musical instruments.

PRUNE de quelque sorte que ce soit

PLUM OF ANY KIND

The more I see you, the more I desire you   3/49 • 4/71

QUEUES DE RENARD

IDENTITY UNCERTAIN

Malice and finesse   3/49 • 4/71

A lot of plants have been dubbed 'queue de renard' ('tail of a fox'). These include Alopecurus myosuroides (large foxtail), Amaranthus viridis (green amaranth) and Equisetum arvense (common horsetail).

RAVE ou REIFFORT

WILD RADISH   (Raphanus raphanistrum)

Don't bother me   3/49 • 4/71

See also: RAVENELLE

A troublesome weed, this has been found growing in cornfields throughout Europe.

RAVENELLE

WILD RADISH   (Raphanus raphanistrum)

Var: Ravanelle, Ravanelle ou ruse

See also: RAVE ou REIFFORT

Out of laziness comes poverty   1/58 • 2/25 • 3/49 • 4/71

REGELICE

LIQUORICE   (Glycyrrhiza glabra)

Var: Reglice

Hidden and attractive sweetness   3/49 • 4/71

Glycyrrhiza glabra is a herbaceous perennial that can grow to a height of 40 inches. Liquorice flavouring is extracted from the root. In ancient China the plant was believed to have magical powers and was the Viagra of the day. In ancient Greece it was incorporated into many types of medication.

REJOINTE ou HERBE À CHARPENTIER

YARROW   (Achillea millefolium)

Come back in friendship   3/49 • 4/71

See also: ACILLETS & MILLE FUEILLE

REMBERGE

MERCURY   (Mercurialis annua)

Var: Remberger

I don't care about you   1/58 • 3/49

Mercury is an annual herb belonging to the spurge family. It can grow to a height of about 27 inches.

RESPONCES

RAMPION   (Campanula rapunculus or Phyteuma)

Don't despise me   3/49 • 4/71

Rampion is the name given to Campanula rapunculus (known both as rampion and as rampion bellflower) and also to several species of Phyteuma including the blue flowered round rampion (P. orbiculare).

RIEBLE

CLEAVERS, GOOSE GRASS   (Galium aparine)

Var: Rioble

You surprised me   1/58

Take it all in your stride   3/49 • 4/71

Cleavers is covered with hairs and prickles to allow it to cling to almost anything it comes in contact with. It can grow to 10 feet tall by climbing up other plants.

RONCE

BRAMBLE   (Rubus)

Black malice   3/49 • 4/71

There are numerous species of bramble, including R. fructicosus (common bramble), R. caesius (dewberry) and R. chaemaemorus (cloudberry). Most have woody stems and thorns, and all have edible fruits.

RONCE SANS ESPINE, la fleur de

BRAMBLE FLOWER WITHOUT A THORN

There is no deception   3/49 • 4/71

ROSE, bouton double de

TWO ROSEBUDS

Opportunity   1/58 • 2/25

ROSE BLANCHE

WHITE ROSE

I'm willing   1/58 • 2/25 • 3/49 • 4/71

ROSE BLANCHE, le bouton

WHITE ROSEBUD

I love you   1/58 • 2/25 • 3/49 • 4/71

It is interesting to note that, whereas nowadays it is the red rose that tends to signify love, in the 16th and 17th centuries it was the white rosebud.

ROSE ROUGE

RED ROSE

Generosity   1/58 • 2/25 • 3/49 • 4/71

ROSE ROUGE, le bouton

SINGLE RED ROSEBUD

Var: Rose rouge, bouton seul de

Anguish   1/58 • 3/49 • 4/71

I have great pain and anguish 4/71

ROSE ROUGE, bouton double de

TWO RED ROSEBUDS

Take the opportunity   3/49 • 4/71

ROSE ROUGE, plusieurs boutons

SEVERAL RED ROSEBUDS

To look for the right opportunity   3/49 • 4/71

ROSE DE PROVINS

FRENCH ROSE, APOTHECARY ROSE   (Rosa gallica)

Be secretive   1/58 • 3/49 • 4/71

Be somewhere else   X1/64

The French rose was one of the first species of rose to be cultivated in Europe. It has sweetly scented dark pink flowers.

ROSE MUSQUÉE

MUSK ROSE   (Rosa moschata)

I refuse you   1/58 • 2/25 • 3/49 • 4/71

The musk rose originated in North Africa. It is a rambler, growing to about 10 feet high and producing large clusters of white flowers. Attar of roses, an essential oil used in perfumes, is distilled from its petals.

ROSEAU

REED

Fickle love   3/49 • 4/71

See also: CANNES

ROSIER, fueille de

LEAF OF ROSEBUSH

Take from somewhere else   1/58 • 2/25

Contemplate something else   3/49 • 4/71

ROSMARIN COUPÉ

ROSEMARY, CUT   (Salvia rosmarinus)

Var: Romarin couppé

Love without end   1/58 • 2/25 • 3/49 • 4/71

A native of the Mediterranean region, wild rosemary is found growing in dry areas and among rocks. Students in ancient Greece, believing it improved the memory, put sprigs of it in their hair while they studied. Shakespeare's 'rosemary for remembrance' probably relates to this belief.

ROSMARIN NON COUPÉ

ROSEMARY, UNCUT

Var: Romarin non couppé

Leave (or **Vacation**)   1/58 • 2/25

I give you leave   3/49 • 4/71

ROUX

NOT IDENTIFIED

Misfortune   3/49 • 4/71

Although 'roux' used as an adjective can mean 'ginger', sadly I have been unable to find anything to indicate that it can also be used as a noun to describe the herb of that name, and no other possibilities have presented themselves.

RUBARBE

RHUBARB   (Rheum rhabarbarum)

Don't be afraid   3/49 • 4/71

Rhubarb was used medicinally for many centuries before its culinary possibilities were recognised. It is said to have been brought to Europe in the 13th century by Marco Polo, but an edible species was only introduced in the early 17th century.

RUBY

RED MADDER   (Rubia tinctorum)

Var: Rudy

Don't fear to leave   1/58

Fear nothing   3/49 • 4/71

A herbaceous perennial, red madder grows to a height of about 4 feet and has dense clusters of small pale yellow flowers. For many centuries its root was used to make a red dye for cloth.

RUE

RUE   (Ruta graveolens)

I don't love you   1/58 • 2/25 • 3/49 • 4/71

An aromatic perennial herb, rue has bluish grey leaves and small yellow flowers. The ancient Greeks used it both medicinally and as a seasoning for food.

SAFFRAN, la feüille de
SAFFRON LEAF   (Crocus sativus)
A little, enough   3/49 • 4/71

The leaves of the saffron or autumn crocus appear much later than its pink flowers (which is why one of the English names for the plant is 'naked ladies'). Its bright crimson stigma and styles (the centre of the flower) have been used in food as colouring and as a spice since ancient times.

SAFFRAN FLEURY
FLOWERING SAFFRON
Enjoyment   3/49 • 4/71

SAPIN
FIR TREE   (Abies)
Grandeur and support   3/49 • 4/71

Long before they became known as Christmas trees, fir trees were used by the Romans to decorate their temples for the winter festival of Saturnalia. Elsewhere, pagans would take fir branches into their homes at the winter solstice as a sign of the spring to come. The first recorded

Christmas tree was erected in 1510 in the town square in Riga, Latvia.

SAUGE
SAGE   (Salvia officinalis)
Sterility   1/58
A short-lived perennial shrub, sage has greyish leaves and flowers whose colour is anywhere between blue and pinkish mauve. It is native to the northern Mediterranean region and was considered sacred by the Romans. It has been used medicinally and in cooking for centuries.

SAUGE FLEURIE
FLOWERING SAGE
I desire to see you   3/49 • 4/71

SAUGE GROSSE
LARGE SAGE
Var: Sauge de la plus grosse
Enterprise   1/58 • 2/25 • 3/49 • 4/71

SAUGE MENUE
SMALL SAGE
Chastity   1/58 • 2/25
Chastity and health   3/49 • 4/71

SAULE, une branche de
WILLOW BRANCH   (Salix)
I don't want you   3/49 • 4/71
See also: OSIER

SAULDRE BLANCHE

WHITE WILLOW   (Salix alba)

False love   3/49 • 4/71

See also: SAULDRE COMMUNE ou VERDE

Salix alba, the white willow, is native to Europe and can grow to a height of 100 feet.

SAULDRE COMMUNE ou VERDE

WHITE WILLOW   (Salix alba)

Sterility   3/49 • 4/71

See also: SAULDRE BLANCHE

SAVIGNY

*SABIN TREE   (Juniperus sabina)

You are pleasant to someone's face but abuse him behind his back   [the original is an idiom: vous mordez en riant]   3/49 • 4/71

Juniperus sabina is an evergreen conifer, native to the mountains of central and southern Europe. It is found at altitudes of 3,000 to 11,000 feet and, in the wild, usually grows to about 6 feet tall, while spreading up to 10 feet wide.

SCABIEUSE

SCABIOUS   (Scabiosa)

Misfortune (or **Unhappiness**)   1/58 • 2/25 • 3/49 • 4/71

There are numerous species of scabious. Most have multi-petalled bluish-purple flowers, although a few are white or pink. Its name is derived from the Latin 'scabiosus' meaning 'itchy'. In the past, the plant has been used medicinally to treat the skin complaint, scabies.

SCALOPENDRE

HART'S TONGUE FERN   (Asplenium scolopendrium)

Finesse   3/49 • 4/71

SEE ALSO: FOUGERE

This is an evergreen fern which has rosettes of strap-like, wavy-edged fronds that can be up to 30 inches long.

SCARIOLLE ou CICOREE

PRICKLY LETTUCE   (Lactuca serriola)

or CHICORY   (Cichorium intybus)

Var: Scariole (with Cicorée as a separate entry)

Riches   1/58

Withdraw completely   3/49 • 4/71

See also: CICORÉE

The prickly lettuce has small spines along the edges of its leaves and a slightly unpleasant smell. It is found in orchards and fields and along the side of roads. Growing to about six feet in height, it produces small yellow flowers. Chicory can grow almost as tall and has bright blue daisy-like flowers.

SEGUE

HEMLOCK   (Conium maculatum)

or WATER HEMLOCK   (Cicuta virosa)

Withdraw from everything   1/58

Withdraw   3/49 • 4/71

Hemlock can grow to a height of 8 feet and has flat-topped clusters of small white flowers. Water hemlock has small umbrella-like clusters of white flowers and can grow to about 6 feet. Both plants are poisonous.

SENESSON

RAGWORT   (Senecio jacobaea)

or GROUNDSEL   (Senecio vulgaris)

Inconstancy   1/58 • 2/25 • 3/49 • 4/71

Ragwort and groundsel are closely related species and both produce small yellow daisy-like flowers in dense clusters.

SENEVÉ

MUSTARD   (Sinapis)

Bad grace   3/49 • 4/71

This may relate to yellow mustard (S. alba), whose seeds are used to make the condiment, black mustard (S. nigra) whose seeds are used as a spice, or wild mustard (S. arvensis). During the Irish potato famine in the early 19th century, the leaves of wild mustard were frequently eaten as a vegetable.

SERPENTINE ou COULEUVRE

SNAKEROOT, SNAKEWEED, ADDERWORT   (Polygonum bistorta)

Prudence   3/49 • 4/71

Snakeroot grows in wet soils and gets its name from the twisted shape of its roots. It produces dense spikes of pale pink flowers.

SERRIETTE

SUMMER SAVORY   (Satureia hortensis)

No one is too good   1/58 • 2/25 • 3/49 • 4/71

This herb has long pointed aromatic leaves and spikes of small lilac-coloured flowers.

SICOMORRE

SYCAMORE   (Acer pseudoplatanus)

To become large from small   3/49 • 4/71

See also: ERABLE

Before earthenware crockery became the norm for tablewares, sycamore wood was often used to make bowls and dishes. The wood, which is soft and white, has also been used over the centuries to create larger items such as carts and ploughs.

SOUCIE, un seul brain

MARIGOLD, ONE STEM   (Calendula officinalis)

Hard to bear   1/58 • 2/25

The marigold has been cultivated for many centuries and, by the 13th century, was being used for both culinary and medical purposes. A cordial made from marigolds was said to cure depression.

SOUCIE, plusieurs brins

MARIGOLD, SEVERAL STEMS

Var: Soucy, plusieurs brins

Alliances (or **Wedding ring**s)   [alliances]   1/58 • 2/25

Alliance   [alliance]   3/49 • 4/71

SOYE, fleur de

SILK FLOWERS

I desire to see you   3/49 • 4/71

The practice of making artificial flowers out of silk began around 500 CE in China. By the 12th century the craft had spread to Italy and, shortly thereafter, to France. By the 15th century, French silk flowers were considered to be the finest in the world.

STRAGON

TARRAGON　　(Artemisia dracunculus)

Promptness and haste　　3/49 • 4/71

A bushy perennial, tarragon originated in Asia but, for centuries, it has been cultivated in Europe. Its leaves are used to flavour vinegar, pickles and French mustard.

SUCRIN, la feüille de

BUTTERNUT SQUASH LEAF　　(Cucurbita moschata)

Var: Suerin

Sure alliance　　3/49 • 4/71

Sucrine translates as butternut squash. However, this is native to Martinique and, although Columbus landed there in 1502, the island was only claimed by the French in 1635. So, when Les Oracles Divertissans was written in 1649, butternut squash would probably have been a very recent import to France and, more than likely, something only available to the wealthy.

SUS

MEANING UNCERTAIN

Var: Sueur, Suc

Despair　　1/58 • 2/25 • 3/49 • 4/71

A literal translation of sus is 'juice' and of sueur is 'sweat'. It is possible that this may relate to water sprayed onto a bouquet – but that's just a guess!

TENASIE

TANSY   (Tanacetum vulgare)

Var: Tenaisie

It does not belong to you   1/58 • 3/49 • 4/71

It does not match you   X1/64

An aromatic plant that produces flat-topped clusters of small yellow flowers, tansy has been grown in gardens since mediaeval times.

TETINE DE CHAT ou DE SOURIS

BITING STONECROP   (Sedum acre)

Without concealing anything   3/49 • 4/71

The biting (or mossy) stonecrop is commonly found growing on walls or on the roofs of houses and in dry sandy soils. It grows only to about 6 inches tall and produces yellow star-shaped flowers.

TIGNE ou PODAGRE DE LIN ou DE LANDE

DODDER   (Cuscuta)

A troubled household   3/49 • 4/71

This parasitic plant can be found growing on brambles, thistles, ferns, hops, nettles and other plants. It has long, thin, yellow or red stems and produces groups of very small pink flowers.

TIM COUPPÉ

THYME, CUT   (Thymus)

You will succeed   1/58 • 2/25 • 3/49 • 4/71

There are many species of thyme including common, or garden, thyme (T. vulgaris) and wild thyme (T. serpyllum). The ancient Egyptians used thyme for embalming, while the ancient Greeks burned it as incense. The Romans used it to flavour cheese and believed it to be an antidote to poisoning. It has been used in cookery since the Middle Ages when it was also thought to offer protection against plague.

TIM NON COUPPÉ

THYME, UNCUT

Perseverance   1/58 • 2/25 • 3/49 • 4/71

TIM, fleur de

THYME FLOWER

Var: Tim fleury

I give myself to you   1/58 • 2/25 • 3/49 • 4/71

TREFFLE

CLOVER, TREFOIL   (Trifolium)

Comfort   1/58 • 2/25 • 3/49 • 4/71

Many species of clover are to be found growing wild in Europe including red clover (T. pratense), meadow trefoil (T. medium), white clover (T. repens), wood trefoil (T. sylvaticum) and sea clover (T. maritimum).

TREMBLE

ASPEN   (Populus tremula)

Respond wisely   3/49 • 4/71

Aspens are members of the poplar family and can grow to a height of 130 feet. Their leaves, which are a coppery colour before they turn green, flutter very easily because the leaf stalks are flattened and flexible. Legend says that the leaves tremble from shame and sorrow because Christ's cross was made from aspen wood.

TULIPLE

TULIP   (Tulipa)

Var: Tulipe

You are beautiful, without spirit & inconstant   3/49 • 4/71

The wild tulip (T. sylvestris) possibly originated in Iran. However, by the start of the 16th century it was being cultivated in Turkey. The Holy Roman Emperor Ferdinand I is said to have been sent tulip seeds by his ambassador to Turkey in 1554. Five years later tulips were being grown in a private garden in Augsburg in Germany.

VALERIENNE

VALERIAN   (Valeriana)

I am looking for you to be my friend   3/49 • 4/71

There are many species of valerian. The European ones include common valerian (V. officinalis), mountain valerian (V. montana), alpine valerian (V. saxatilis) and marsh valerian (V. dioica). All have clusters of white or pink flowers, and those of the common valerian are sweetly scented.

VERGE À PASTEUR

SMALL TEASEL   (Dipsacus pilosus)

Theft   3/49 • 4/71

The small teasel can be found throughout Europe in woods and hedges. It grows to a height of 5 feet and puts out dense spherical, greenish flower heads that are up to an inch across.

VERGE DE BOULLAZ PELLÉE

*BIRCH ROD

Var: Verge de boulas pelée

Our case is discovered   1/58

Our business (or **affair**) **is discovered**   3/49 • 4/71

'Boullaz' may be 'boulay', which translates as birch tree, while 'pelée' means 'peeled'.

VERMINEUSE

PURPLE MULLEIN   (Verbascum phoeniceum)

Someone else has taken the place   3/49 • 4/71

See also: MOLAINE

The purple mullein is native to southern Europe and is to be found growing on the edges of woods and in stony grassy fields. It produces spikes of saucer-shaped flowers, the lowest of which open first.

VERVAINE

VERVAIN   (Verbena)

Don't leave me for someone else   3/49 • 4/71

A perennial herb, with spikes of small pink or purple flowers, vervain has been used medicinally since Roman times and, for many years was believed to be a protection against black magic.

VIGNE

GRAPEVINE   (Vitis vinifera)

A reason for everything   1/58 • 2/25 • 3/49 • 4/71

The grapevine was probably first cultivated in Mesopotamia between 7000 and 4000 BCE. From there it spread to the Middle East and to Europe. There is evidence to suggest that grapes were being turned into wine by 6000 BCE. In France, the cultivation of vines together with wine-making probably began around 600 BCE.

VIGNE, pampre de
VINE BRANCH WITH YOUNG LEAVES
Jubilation and recreation   3/49 • 4/71

VIGNE, le clavicule de la
MEANING OF 'CLAVICULE' UNCERTAIN
Don't keep me in suspense   1/58

VINELLE ou VIGNE AU CRAPAUT
**TOAD SORREL
Why don't you get married?   3/49 • 4/71
The identification of this as toad sorrel is something of a guess.
'Crapaut' translates as 'toad' while 'vinette' (not 'vinelle') is a name for
sorrel (it is also a name for the barberry – see below). More than one
species of Oxalis (wood sorrel) has been given the name of toad sorrel in
English but, if this is the correct interpretation here, it probably relates
to Oxalis europea which grows in damp woodland and produces yellow
flowers.

VINETTE GROSSE ou TRINCHON
LARGE BARBERRY   (Berberis vulgaris)
Reparation   3/49 • 4/71
The common barberry is the only species of Berberis native to Europe.
It grows in hedges and coppices and likes chalky soil. A shrub that
can grow to 10 feet tall, it has spiny stems and drooping yellow flowers
followed by bright red berries.

VINETTE MENUË
SMALL BARBERRY
Ease my ardent desire   3/49 • 4/71

VINETTE, feüille de
BARBERRY LEAF
Certainty of love   3/49 • 4/71

VIOLET ou DAMAS VIOLET
DAMASK VIOLET   (Hesperis matronalis)
I will help you   3/49 • 4/71

The damask violet or dame's rocket was possibly first cultivated in
France in the 15th century. Its flowers are white or purple and its sweet
fragrance is particularly noticeable in the evening.

VIOLETTE DE MARS
SWEET VIOLET   (Viola odorata)
Var: Violette de mars, feuille de [Sweet violet leaf]
Don't trouble yourself   1/58 • 2/25 • 3/49 • 4/71

Viola martia is an old name for Viola odorata. Native to Europe, it is
recorded as being grown by specialist nurseries in ancient Greece and sold
in the markets of Athens. It was a very common garden flower during
the Middle Ages.

VIOLETTE DE MARS BLANCHE
WHITE VIOLET
Var: Violette blanche
Good hope   1/58 • 2/25 • 3/49 • 4/71

VIOLETTE DE MARS DOUBLE

DOUBLE VIOLET

Wanting to declare (himself)   1/58 • 2/25

Hidden and secret love   3/49 • 4/71

VIOLETTES DE MARS DOUBLES, plusieurs ensemble

BUNCH OF DOUBLE VIOLETS

Var: Viollettes . . .

I want to declare myself   3/49 • 4/71

VIOLETTE DE MARS SIMPLE ET BLEUE

BLUE SINGLE VIOLET

Concealed sorrow   1/58

VIOLET GRIS

GREY VIOLET

Help me   3/49 • 4/71

VIOLETTE AYANT LE PIED PELU

VIOLET WITH A HAIRY FOOT

Var: Violette avant le pied velu (also meaning 'hairy')

False pretences   1/58 • 3/49 • 4/71

VIOLETTE D'OUTRE MER

*BLUE VIOLET

Patience   1/58 • 3/49 • 4/71

'D'outre mer' translates as 'Indian blue', which is a mid to light shade
of blue.

VIOLETTE D'YVER

WINTER VIOLET

Var: Violette d'hyver

Lost time 1/58 • 2/25 • 3/49 • 4/71

VIOLIER BLANC

WHITE HOARY STOCK

Var: Violet blanc (probably a misprint)

See also: GIROFLÉE BLANCHE

In a bold heart and perfect agreement 1/58

A bold heart and perfect agreement 2/25

Pure heart and honest agreement 3/49 • 4/71

VIOLIER ROUGE

RED HOARY STOCK

Var: Violet rouge (probably a misprint)

See also: GIROFLEE ROUGE

Concealed love 1/58 • 2/25 • 3/49 • 4/71

YF

YEW   (Taxus baccata)

Var: If, Yr

Consumption of goods   1/58 • 3/49 • 4/71

Yew wood is exceptionally strong and durable. One of the oldest surviving wooden artefacts in the world, a spear head made of yew, is thought to be about 450,000 years old. Yew has also been used to make longbows, tool handles and furniture. Every part of the tree is poisonous.

YSOPE

HYSSOP   (Hyssopus officinalis)

Bitterness   1/58 • 2/25 • 3/49 • 4/71

A shrub with fragrant pink, blue or, less often, white flowers, hyssop has been used medicinally for many centuries. 'Hyssop' is mentioned in the Bible but it is uncertain whether this refers to today's common hyssop, H. officinalis, or another plant entirely.

YVRAYE

RYEGRASS   (Lolium)

Harmful food   3/49 • 4/71

There are a number of species of ryegrass native to Europe including annual ryegrass (L. multiflorum) and perennial ryegrass (L. perenne).

ENGLISH-FRENCH INDEX OF FLOWER NAMES

Acer . . . . .Erable

Agrimony . . . . Aigremoine

Alder buckthorn . . . . Bourdaine

Alecost .Coq

Alkanet . . . . Buglosse

Almond . . . . .Amandier

– blossom . . . . .Amandier, la fleur d'

Aloes . . . . Aloyes fleuries

Amaranth . . . . .Amarante

– green . . . . Passe veloux

Aniseed . . . . .Anis

Apple . . . . .Pomme

– tree . . . . Pommier

Apricot . . . . Abricot

– tree . . . . Abricotier

– blossom . . . . Abricotier, la fleur d'

Ash tree . . . . .Fresne

Asparagus . . . . Asperges

Aspen . . . . Tremble

Bachelor's button . . . . Bleuvette perce

Balm, common . . . . .Bausme; Pimant

Barberry. . . . . .Vinette grosse ou Trinchon; Vinette menuë

– leaf . . . . .Vinette, feüille de

Barley, ear of . . . . Espy d'orge

Basil . . . . .Baselic

Bastard chamomile . . . . . .Maroüet

Bay . . . . Laurier

Bean

– leaf . . . . .Febue, feüille de

– flower . . . . Febue, fleur de;Feues, fleur de

– pod . . . . Febue, la gousse de

Beech

– tree . . . . .Fouteau

– nuts . . . . Foine ou Graine de fousteau

Beetroot . . . . Bette rouge

Betony . . . . Betoyne

Birch rod . . . . Verge de boullaz pellée

Black vanilla orchid . . . . .Jalousie

Blackthorn . . . . .Espine noire fleurie

Blessed thistle herb . . . . . .Chardon benist

Borage . . . . .Bourache

Box . . . . Buis

Box-holly . . . . Fresgon

– berry . . . . Fresgon, la greine de

Bracken . . . . .Fougere

Bramble . . . . .Ronce

– flower . . . . .Ronce sans espine, la fleur de

Brome . . . . Brome

Broom . . . . .Genest

– berry . . . . .Genest, la graine de

– flower . . . . .Genest, fleur de

Buckthorn .Espine noire fleurie

Bugleweed .Patte de loup

Bugloss, common . . . . .Buglosse

Burnet . . . . Pimpenelle

Butternut squash leaf . . . . .Sucrin, la feüille de

Cabbage leaf . . . . Chou, la feuille

Cannabis . . . . Chanvre

Caper spurge . . . . .Epeurge

Carrots . . . . .Karottes; Pastonnades ou Carottes

Castor oil plant . . . . .Palme christi

Cauliflower . . . . Chou, la fleur

Cedar . . . . Cedre

Celery . . . . .Ache

Chamomile .Camomille

Chanterelle . . . . Jaunerotes

Chard, white . . . . .Bette blanche

Cherry tree . . . . Ceresier

Chervil . . . . .Cerfueil

Chestnut

– tree . . . . Chastaigne & son herisson

– leaf . . . . Chastaigner, fueille de

– nut . . . . Chastaigne & son herisson

Chickweed .Morron

Chicory . . . . Cicorée; Scariolle ou Cicoree

Chinese lantern . . . . .Carchanges

Chives . . . . .Cive

Cleavers . . . . Rieble

Clover . . . . .Treffle

Columbine .Ancolie; Encolie

Coriander .Coriande

Corn cockle . . . . .Nielle

Cornflower . . . . Bleuvette perce

– violet . . . . .Bleuvette violette

Costmary . . . . .Coq

Couchgrass . . . . Chien-dent

Cowslip . . . . Primevere

Crabgrass . . . . .Millet

Cranesbill

– herb Robert . . . . Changre ou Herbe robert

– red . . . . Changre rouge, fleur de

– azure . . . . .Changre azurée, fleur de

Cress, garden . . . . .Cresson de jardin

Crown imperial . . . . Couronne imperialle

Cuckoo pint . . . . Giron

Currant . . . . Groselier

– red . . . . ,Groisillier rouge

Daffodil . . . . Narcisse ou Fleur de janvier

Daisy . . . . Margrites

– field . . . . .Margrite champestre

– grey . . . . Marguerite grise

– ox eye . . . . .Margrite blanche

– red . . . . .Marguerite rouge

– single . . . . .Margrite seule

Dandelion flower . . . . Dent de lion, fleur de

Danewort . . . . Hieble

Day lily, yellow . . . . .Lys jaune

Gorse . . . . .Lande

– flowering . . . . .Lande fleurie

Grapevine . . . . .Vigne

Grass . . . . .Herbe commune

– flowering . . . . .Herbe fleurie

Greater celandine . . . . Esclere ou Celidoine

Ground ivy . . . . .Herbe S. Jean ou Lierre terrestre

Groundsel . . . . Senesson

Gypsyflower . . . . .Langue de chien

Hairy woodrush . . . . Langue de pivert, fleur de

Hart's tongue fern . . . . . . .Scalopendre

Hawthorn . . . . .Aubespine fleurie; Espine blanche

– flowering . . . . Espine blanche fleurie

Hazel . . . . Couldre

– nuts . . . . .Couldre; Noisillier, les noisettes du

Heal-all . . . . Brunette

Heather . . . . .Bruere

Hellebore . . . . Ellebore

Hemlock . . . . .Segue

Herb-bennet . . . . Galiot

Herb robert . . . . Changre ou Herbe Robert

Hogweed . . . . .Patte d'ours

Holly . . . . Houx

– berry . . . . .Houx, graine de

Hollyhock . . . . .Passe rose

– white . . . . Passe-rose blanche

Honesty . . . . .Lunaire

Honeysuckle . . . . .Chevre-feuil

– purple . . . . .Pentecouste violette, la fleur de

– red . . . . .Pentecouste rouge, la fleur de

– white . . . . .Pentecouste blanche, la fleur de

Honeywort . . . . Melineuf

Hops . . . . Houblon

Horehound . . . . Mente blanche

Houseleek . . . . .Jobarde

Hyacinth bluebell . . . . .Hyacinte

Hyacinth . . . . Hyacinte

Hyssop . . . . .Ysope

Iris, bearded . . . . .Flambe ou Iris, fleur de

Ivy . . . . Lyerre

Juniper . . . . Genevre

Knotgrass . . . . Herbe noüée d'un noeud ou de plusieurs

Larkspur . . . . .Pied d'alouette

Laurel . . . . Laurier

– berry of . . . . Laurier, graine de

– leaves & branches . . . . . . Laurier, les feüilles et rinceaux de

– leaf of cut . . . . Laurier couppée, fueille de

Lavender cotton . . . . Lavande cotonnée

Lavender . . . . Lavande

Leek . . . . Porée ou Poreaux

Lemon balm . . . . .Bausme; Pimant

Lettuce . . . . , , Lectue

Lilac chaste tree . . . . .Muguet bleu

Lily . . . . Lys

– leaf . . . . .Lys, la feüille de

Lily of the valley . . . . Lys de vallée; Muguet

Ling . . . . Bruere

Linseed . . . . .Lin

Liquorice . . . . Regelice

Lords and ladies . . . . .Giron

Lovage . . . . Lyvesche

Love-lies-bleeding . . . . Amaranth

Madonna lily . . . . Lys blanche, la fleur de

Maidenhair fern . . . . .Adiantos; Capilli veneris

Mallow . . . . Maulves, fleur de

Mandrake . . . . Mandragore

Maple . . . . .Erable

Marigold

– one stem . . . . Soucie, un seul brain

– several stems . . . . Soucie, plusieurs brins

Marjoram . . . . Marjolaine grosse; Marjolaine menue

Mastic tree . . . . Mastic

Mayweed . . . . .Amaroufle

Medlar . . . . .Mellier

Mercury . . . . Remberge

Milk thistle . . . . .Lettrons

Millet . . . . Millet

Mimosa . . . . Herbe sensitive

Mint . . . . Mante; Mentastre ou Mente sauvage

– apple . . . . .Mente blanche

– black . . . . .Mente noire

– water . . . . .Mente aquatique

– wild . . . . .Mentastre ou Mente sauvage

Mistletoe . . . . Guy

– berry . . . . .Gui, graine de

Moss

– green . . . . .Mousse verde

Pansies, bunch of . . . . . . Pensées, bouquet de plusieurs

Parsley . . . . .Persil

Parsnip . . . . Panais

Parsnips . . . . Pastonnades ou Carottes

Pea

– flower . . . . .Poix, fleur de

– leaf . . . . Pois, feüilles de

– pod . . . . Poix, gousse de

Peach . . . . Pesche

– blossom . . . . Pescher, fleur de

Pear

– tree . . . . Poirier

– wild . . . . .Poires sauvages

Pellitory . . . . Aparitoire

Pennyroyal . . . . .Polliot

Periwinkle . . . . Espervanche

Persicaria . . . . Cuyrage

Petty whin . . . . .Escloppe chien

Pine

– tree . . . . Pin

– needles . . . . Pin, feüilles de

Pineapple . . . . .Pineaux

Pink, garden . . . . Herminettes

– leaf of . . . . Oeillet, feüille d'

Plantain . . . . Plantain

Plum . . . . .Prune de quelque sorte que ce soit

– tree . . . . .Prunier

Polypody, common . . . . . Pollipode

Poppy

– red . . . . .Pavot rouge, la fleur de

– white . . . . .Pavot blanc, la fleur de

Prickly lettuce . . . . .Scariolle ou Cicoree

Primrose . . . . Primevere

Primula . . . . Primevere

Pumpkin . . . . Cytreulle; Potiron

Purslane . . . . .Pourpie

Quince . . . . Coigner

Radish, wild . . . . .Rave ou Reiffort; Ravenelle

Ragwort . . . . .Senesson

Rampion . . . . .Responces

Raspberry . . . . Franboyse

Red shank . . . . Cuyrage

Red madder . . . . .Ruby

Reed . . . . Cannes; Roseau

Rhubarb . . . . Rubarbe

Rose

– apothecary . . . . Rose de provins

– briar . . . . Esglantier

– dog . . . . Esglantier; Esglantier, rose d'

– French . . . . Rose de provins

– musk . . . . .Rose musquée

– red . . . . .Rose rouge

– white . . . . .Rose blanche

– wild . . . . .Esglantier

Rosebud(s)

– single red . . . . .Rose rouge, le bouton

– several red . . . . .Rose rouge, plusieurs boutons

– two red . . . . .Rose rouge, bouton double de

– two . . . . .Rose, bouton double de

– white . . . . Rose blanche, le bouton

Rosebush, leaf of . . . . .Rosier, fueille de

Rose daphne . . . . Laureolle

Rosemary

– cut .Rosmarin coupé

– uncut . . . . Rosmarin non coupé

Rue . . . . .Rue

Rush

– one stem . . . . Jonc, un brin de

– two stems . . . . Jonc, deux brins de

Ryegrass . . . . Yvraye

Sabin tree . . . . Savigny

Saffron

– flowering . . . . .Saffran fleury

– leaf . . . . Saffran, la feüille de

Sage . . . . Sauge; Sauge grosse; Sauge menue

– flowering . . . . Sauge fleurie

Samphire . . . . .Percepierre

Scabious . . . . .Scabieuse

– devil's bit (false) . . . . Morsure du diable ou Faulse scabieuse

Scaly spleenwort . . . . .Ceterac

Scarlet pimpernel . . . . .Morron

Self-heal . . . . .Brunette

Sensitive plant . . . . .Herbe sensitive

Service tree . . . . Cormier

Silk flowers . . . . Soye, fleur de

Silverweed . . . . Argentine

Skirret . . . . .Eschervis

Small teasel . . . . .Verge à pasteur

Snakeroot . . . . .Serpentine ou Couleuvre

Snow in summer . . . . Argentine

Sorrel

– field . . . . .Oseille ou Vinette menue

– large . . . . .Oseille grosse

– sheep . . . . .Oseille ou Vinette menue

Sow thistle . . . . .Lettrons

Spider orchid . . . . .Bourdon de giron

Spike lavender . . . . .Aspic

– leaf of . . . . Aspic, feuille d'

Spinach . . . . Espinars

Spindle tree . . . . Guaras

Spurge . . . . .Laict au cocu

Spurge laurel . . . . Aureolle; Laureolle

St John's wort . . . . Mille-pertuis

Stinking chamomile . . . . .Amaroufle

Stinking hellebore . . . . .Patte d'ours

Stock

– grey . . . . .Girofflée grise

– red . . . . .Giroflée rouge; Violier rouge

– white . . . . Giroflée blanche; Violier blanc

Stonecrop, biting . . . . .Tetine de chat ou de souris

Straw or stem . . . . .Piccourt ou Ranicule

Strawberry . . . . Fraise ou la fleur

– flower . . . . Fraise ou la fleur

– leaf . . . . .Fraisier, la feüille de

Summer savory . . . . Serriette

Swine cress . . . . Corne de cerf

Swiss chard . . . . .Bette blanche

Sycamore . . . . .Sicomorre

Tansy . . . . .Tenasie

Tarragon . . . . Stragon

Thistle . . . . Chardon

Thorn . . . . .Espine

Thyme

– cut . . . . .Tim couppé

– flower . . . . Tim, fleur de

– uncut . . . . Tim non couppé

Toad sorrel . . . . .Vinelle ou Vigne au crapaut

Trefoil . . . . Treffle

Tulip . . . . Tuliple

Turk's cap lily . . . . Martagon

Turnip . . . . Naveau

Valerian . . . . Valerienne

Vervain . . . . .Vervaine

Vine branch with leaves . . . . .Vigne, pampre de

Violet

– blue . . . . Violette d'outre mer

– blue single . . . . Violette de mars simple et bleue

– damask .Violet ou Damas violet

– double . . . . Violette de mars double

– double, bunch of . . . . .Violettes de mars doubles, plusieurs

– double yellow . . . . .Bassinetz

– grey . . . . Violet gris

– sweet . . . . Violette de mars

– white . . . . Violette de mars blanche

– winter . . . . Violette d'yver

– with a hairy foot . . . . . . .Violette ayant le pied pelu

Wallflower . . . . .Girofflée de prairie ou de muraille

Walnut . . . . Noyer

– leaf . . . . .Noyer, fueille de

Water lily . . . . .Nerprun

– berry . . . . Nerprun, graine de

Water chestnut

– flower . . . . Macre, la fleur de

– fruit of the . . . . Macre, le fruit de

Water crowfoot . . . . .Douves aquatiques

Water hemlock . . . . Segue

Watercress . . . . Cresson d'eau

Wheat

– ear of . . . . Espy de bled; Espy de froment

– empty ear of . . . . Espi de bled vuide

– full ear of . . . . .Espi de bled chargé

– two ears of . . . . .Espy de bled double

– three ears of . . . . Espy de bled triple

Wild service tree . . . . .Allisier

– fruit . . . . .Allisier, le fruit d'

Willow . . . . Osier

– branch . . . . Saule, une branche de

– white . . . . Sauldre blanche; Sauldre commune

Wood avens . . . . Galiot

Wormwood . . . . .Alvisnes

Yarrow . . . . Acillets; Mille fueille; Rejointe

Yew . . . . .Yf

Made in the USA
Monee, IL
04 May 2024

57978454R10098